WHO'S AT FAULT?

WHY AMERICA IS DROWNING IN DEBT

SAM BLACK

Library of Congress Cataloging-in-Publication Data

Black, Sam

Who's at Fault/Sam Black

TXu 2-045-775   2017

COVER DESIGN BY MARIA ARRIVIELLO

TABLE OF CONTENTS

PROLOGUE

Who's at Fault? By Sam Black is about the runaway train carrying our money, not only in Washington, but throughout the United States. This is a non-fiction book filled with unimaginable numbers which show how our country got into this $20 Trillion plus hole and who is to blame for this debacle.

After graduating high school, I enlisted in the United States Air Force. I am a father of two children and a grandfather of four. My entire working career has been spent in sales and sales management. Numbers have always intrigued me.

I hope you enjoy reading this book as much as I enjoyed putting it together for you. Hang onto your boot straps for a journey into a deep, dark hole. Better keep your blood pressure pill handy as you progress through this book—You may need one.

Chapter 1

WARS ARE COSTLY

After the Japanese attacked Pearl Harbor on December 7, 1941, smoke billowed from the USS Arizona.

Declared an official holiday in 1971, Memorial Day honors those who have given their lives in service to the United States. While the human toll is always great, wars also cost our U.S. Treasury.

Many factors can affect the cost of waging war. Using a report from the Congressional Research Service, 24/7 Wall St. reviewed the most expensive wars in U.S. history. While the Mexican-American War cost just $2.4 billion, or 1.4 percent of GDP in 1847, spending on World War II accounted for nearly 36 percent of GDP in 1945, or $4.1 trillion. These are the most expensive wars in U.S. history.

Many early wars in U.S. history resulted in the acquisition of land. The Mexican-American War in the 1840s yielded much of the territory that makes up the present-day Southwest. Similarly, the Spanish-American War prior to the start of the 20th Century ended with U.S. control of Guam, Puerto Rico and the Philippines.

In every conflict before World War II, nearly all of the country's defense budget was spent on direct conflict—classified as wartime spending. For example, the U.S. spent 1.1 percent of GDP in 1899 to fight the Spanish-American War and just 1.5 percent of GDP on total defense spending.

That trend largely changed at the start of the Cold War. The persistent threat of military conflict ensured that the U.S. would be ready for war at any time, as the space race and nuclear armament became national priorities in both the U.S. and the Soviet Union. As a result, wartime spending and defense spending began to diverge. During the Korean War, for example, war costs accounted for just 4.2 percent of GDP in 1952, while total defense spending represented more than 13 percent of GDP that same year.

Comparing war costs over a 235-year period can be difficult. While the report attempted to correct for inflation by calculating each war's cost in fiscal year 2011 dollars, inflation adjustments do not account for advances in technology. It is entirely possible that wars also became more expensive over time as the sophistication and cost of technology increased.

To determine the most expensive wars in U.S. history, 24/7 Wall St. used a 2010 report from the Congressional Research Service titled, "Costs of Major U.S. Wars." The report does not include veterans' benefits, interest on loans used to finance the war and assistance to allies. Additionally, the report attempts to capture the increase in military expenditures during wartime and does not include the costs of maintaining a standing army in peacetime. The report also presents both military costs and defense spending as percentages of GDP in the year of peak war spending. War cost figures for the War on Terror were updated to reflect expenditure after 2010.

1. World War II

Once the U.S. emerged from its isolationist shell, it spent more than $4 trillion fighting in World War II and lost more than 400,000 troops. U.S. involvement officially began on December 8, 1941, the day after the Japanese bombed Pearl Harbor. America officially declared war against Germany and Italy three days later. After conquering a number of European countries, Germany focused its attention on the Soviet Union. By 1944, Soviet forces were successfully driving German troops west. On June 6, 1944, Allied forces landed on the beaches of Normandy, pushing east into Europe, splitting the Germans along two fronts.

In the Pacific, U.S. military experts estimated that an invasion of Japan would likely result in much greater casualties. President Harry Truman ordered an atomic bomb be dropped on Hiroshima on August 6, 1945. At the Yalta Conference months earlier, Stalin had promised to enter the Pacific front within three months of the war's end in Europe. If the Soviets were involved in Japan's defeat, they would likely insist on reparations. To prevent a Soviet claim to Japanese assets, assert U.S.-dominance over Stalin and secure a Japanese surrender, Truman ordered a second atomic bomb be dropped on Nagasaki on August 9, the day after the Soviet Union declared war on Japan. By the end of the war, according to conservative estimates, more than 50 million soldiers and civilians had given their lives.

2. The War on Terror

Conflicts in Iraq and Afghanistan following September 11, 2001—collectively known as the War on Terror—cost the U.S. more than $1.6 trillion through 2010. The U.S. entered Afghanistan in October 2001 to search for Osama bin Laden, the mastermind behind the terrorist attacks in New York and Washington D.C. and to overthrow the Taliban government, which had been long-suspected of harboring terrorists. U.S. troops invaded Iraq and overthrew Saddam Hussein in 2003 operating on the belief that he had weapons of mass destruction. Elections in both Iraq and Afghanistan, as well as training military personnel in each country to help stabilize the region, are both heralded as successes. Despite these successes, both countries continue to be marred by conflict.

After this war was declared over, a good friend of mine, a retired master sergeant and former employee, was sent over to the land of desert storm to dismantle all firing pins from army tanks and machine guns. The federal government bought caterpillar bulldozers and sent them to the land of sand to bury several million dollars-worth of equipment. Too costly to ship them back to the states. Lobbyists hard at work back in Washington—destroy the old and buy new. Question: what happened to those tanks and machine guns buried in the sand? Did the enemy dig them up and use them against our soldiers?

3. Vietnam War

The war in Vietnam cost the U.S. $738 billion, or just 2.3 percent of GDP in 1968. By the end of the conflict, the names of more than 58,000 dead soldiers were recorded on the Vietnam Veterans Memorial in Washington, D.C. After North Vietnamese troops drove the French out of the region in 1954, ending a brutal era of colonialism, the Geneva Accords stipulated that elections in the South be scheduled for the following year. Determined not to let communism spread, the U.S. lent its support to Ngo Dinh Diem, a French-educated, Catholic politician in South Vietnam. By the time the U.S. committed troops in 1965, Diem had been assassinated and Vietnamese support for the new military-led South Vietnamese government had faded. With supplies from China and the Soviet Union,

North Vietnam primarily used guerilla tactics to attack U.S. troops and bases, often by surprise. By the late 1960s, public support in the U.S. for the war had faded. American troops officially withdrew from the region in 1973 and South Vietnam fell to communism in 1975.

Let us not forget the TROOPS that died from agent orange and are still dying to this day from DDT. If you recall, our government used the spray, "DDT," to kill foliage.

If you are a full-blooded taxpayer living in the U.S., this next sentence will make your blood boil. This first-hand information came from friends of mine who had served in Vietnam.
Hundreds of undamaged U.S. helicopters used in Vietnam were shoved overboard off Navy carriers. Troops were informed it was too costly to ship them home. Again, lobbyists hard at work back in Washington.
Over 10 percent of all combat and combat-support deaths in Vietnam occurred in helicopter operations, a combined total of 6,175 (2,202 pilots, 2,704 aircrew and 1,269 passengers). The U.S. Army accounted for about 86 percent of these casualties. In addition to the human cost, the helicopter "casualties" of the war were staggering. A total of 11,800 helicopters of all types served in Vietnam. Approximately 5,000 helicopters were destroyed there, of which all but 500 were U.S. Army and we LOST THE DAMN WAR, plus the helicopters we shoved into the water.

4. Korean War

In June 1950, the Soviet-supported North Korean military crossed the 38th parallel that divided North and South Korea. Fearful of the spread of communism, President Harry Truman garnered support from allies in the United Nations Security Council to drive the North Korean troops out of the South. General Douglas MacArthur, however, pursued the North Koreans to the Yalu River, which formed the northern border between China and the Korean peninsula. The Chinese interpreted MacArthur's actions as an act of war and routed the U.N. troops, forcing them to retreat below the 38th parallel. The war eventually ended after Dwight Eisenhower assumed the presidency and threatened the use of nuclear weapons if the North Koreans or Chinese did not respect the 38th parallel as the boundary between the two countries.

Ultimately, the Korean War cost the U.S. $341 billion and nearly 34,000 lives. Again, We Lost the Damn War! And look at what we are dealing with in North Korea today.

5. World War I

War broke out in Europe in 1914, but the U.S. remained neutral for the following three years. However, after Germany reneged on its pledge to respect the neutrality of U.S. ships in the Atlantic and tried to entice Mexico into declaring war on the U.S., President Woodrow Wilson asked Congress for a Declaration of War on April 2, 1917. The war ended 19 months later with the Treaty of Versailles. Ultimately, the war cost the U.S. $334 billion, or nearly 14 percent of GDP in 1919.

WE WON THAT WAR!

How many years has the United States been at war since 1776?

America has been at war 93 percent of the Time—**222** out of **239 Years**—since 1776.

It is pretty much true that the U.S. is engaged in some military effort of some sort or another at nearly any given time. These past WARS were extremely costly.

According to a Harvard University's Kennedy School's study dated March 28, 2013, the Afghanistan wars, together, will cost **$4** to **$6 trillion**.

How long will we stay? Somebody is making money in the U.S. while our TROOPS are being killed, wounded or diagnosed with PTSD. We send our TROOPS to fight a war we will never win and then wonder why so many men come home needing psychiatric treatment, another huge slug added to our national debt. Men keep giving their heart and soul to win a war but the WIN never gets posted anywhere. If we go to WAR, then go to WIN, and not come home with nothing but casualties and wounded warriors.

On February 28th, 2017, our current President, President Trump, stated in his speech to the Joint Session of Congress the following: "The next war the U.S. is engaged in—we will come home winners." Sounds like General George S. Patton. Back when men were men. Hope he backs that up. If he doesn't, write him off the next election.

Federal Waste

As of September 2014, the Department of Defense had an estimated "$857 million in excess parts and supplies." This figure has risen over the past years and of the Pentagon waste that has been calculated, two figures especially worth mentioning are the expenditure of "$150 million on private villas for a handful of Pentagon employees in Afghanistan and the procurement of the JLENS air-defense balloon" which, throughout the program's development over the past two decades, is estimated to have cost $2.7 billion. It is important to note that the JLENS air-balloon still does not function properly.

The Pentagon has wasted $28 million on uniforms for Afghan soldiers. Here is how: They took this $28 million from hard-working taxpayers and blew it on forest-color camouflage uniforms picked out by the Afghan Defense Minister, when only 2 percent of Afghanistan territory is forest land. This leaves all soldiers standing out like sitting ducks and telling the enemy shoot me, I'm your pigeon. The defense minister thought the uniforms looked pretty. **Our idiots in the Pentagon went along with it.**

Comparison with other countries

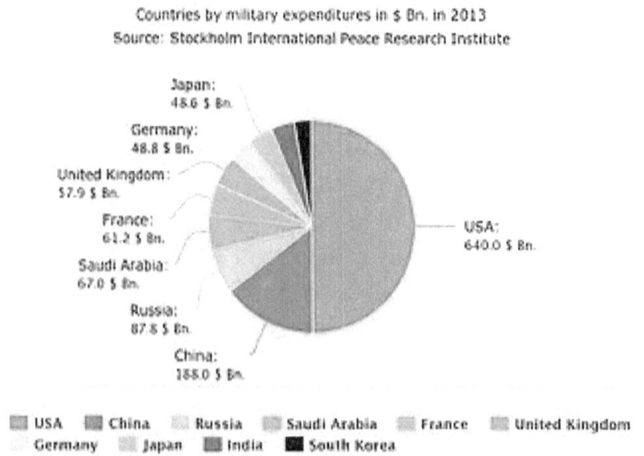

The U.S. military budget is higher than the nine other biggest military budgets in the World combined.

Military Spending as a Percentage of GDP

The United States spends more on their defense budget than China, Saudi Arabia, Russia, United Kingdom, India, France and Japan, combined. The 2009 U.S. military budget accounted for approximately 40 percent of global arms spending. The 2012 budget is six to seven times larger than the $106 billion military budget of China. The United States and its close allies are responsible for two-thirds to three-quarters of the world's military spending (of which, in turn, the U.S. is responsible for the majority). The U.S. also maintains the largest number of military bases on foreign soil across the world. While there are no freestanding foreign bases permanently located in the United States, there are now around 800 U.S. bases in foreign countries. Yet, ISIS is killing people all over the world.

As of March 1, 2017, President Trump has increased our DEFENSE BUDGET by $54 billion. They, the Republicans, cut other expenditures by $54 billion to use on defense. I voted for Trump and have no regrets. Not yet, anyway. I want to see some results from our defense budget—not just DEAD SOLDIERS and WOUNDED SOLDIERS. I want our country to destroy ISIS before this book is printed. Is being bigger better or is being smarter better? What the hell are they going to buy for $54 billion? THE PUBLIC NEEDS ANSWERS!

NEWS ALERT! May 24, 2017. JUST CAME OVER THE TV SCREEN THAT ONE BILLION DOLLARS WORTH OF MILITARY EQUIPMENT, including tanks, ammo, mortars, machine guns, Humvees, etc. were left in Iraq. It is now believed that ISIS has this equipment in their possession and are using it against our Soldiers. A slip-up by the Records Department located in the Pentagon, which employs 23,000 people to make damn sure this kind of thing doesn't happen. I say BULLSHIT! Somebody's ass should be on fire for this so-called mistake. Lobbyists are lying in the weeds waiting for our Defense Department to open up their purse strings.
How many damn lobbyists do the defense contractors have in Washington? I don't understand why we don't shut off ISIS's supply line. Who the hell is feeding them? LOOK ABOVE!! I, also, bet my money on IRAN. No, I don't have any proof. Why were the sanctions on Iran lifted? Why did Obama deliver pallets of CASH to Iran totaling $400 million? A debt owed, they say. I say, bullshit! How about $400,000,000.00 going to thousands of college students whose student loans are up toward $1.1trillion?

Just How Big Is Iran?

Iran is 636,374 square miles (1,629,807 square kilometers), making it the world's seventeenth largest country. Iran is only 4 percent smaller than Alaska, the largest State in the United States.

The limitations of map-making contribute to few of us realizing just how large Alaska is. Maps of the United States frequently show Alaska as an afterthought, small and off to the side, with a different scale from the mainland. However, from the farthest reaches of the Aleutian Islands to Cape Muzon at the foot of the Alexander Archipelago is about as wide as the continental U.S., and at an area of 663,267 square miles (1,717,854 square kilometers), Alaska comprises about 18 percent of the U.S.'s total area.

Iran is dry and mountainous, with broad swaths of desert. With nearly 70,000,000 people, its population is more than one hundred times as dense as Alaska's. Two-thirds of Iranians live in cities. The country's ethnic diversity includes Kurds and Azerbaijanis in the northwest, Arabs in the southwest, and Afghans in the east, in addition to the dominant—but not majority—Persians.

According to the International Energy Agency, Iran pumped 3.64 million barrels of oil per day in May 2016, just four months after sanctions were lifted. That is the fastest pace since June 2011, before tougher sanctions were imposed by the U.S. and other world powers over Iran's nuclear program. Yet, some U.S. companies are gearing up to help Iran with their production output. Greed at its finest. Our own companies helping the enemy. That should not be allowed. If you trust Iran, you'll trust anyone.

MONEY RUNS AHEAD OF COMMON SENSE EVERYDAY IN WASHINGTON

Neighboring Iraq, by comparison, is slightly larger than California, or about a quarter of the size of Iran, at 167,618 square miles (434,128 square kilometers). Iraq's landscape is flatter than Iran's, with mountains largely confined to the north; the rest of the country features desert or fertile areas fed by the Tigris and Euphrates Rivers.

To the east of Iran is Afghanistan. At 249,347 square miles (645,807 square kilometers), it is slightly smaller than Texas (268,581 square miles [695,261 square kilometers]), but it is far more mountainous.

The U.S. hasn't taken any oil out of Iran in years. But China, Japan and many European countries are gobbling up Iran's oil as I type this.

THIS IS ABSOLUTELY WRONG. Shut off their supply lines and let them rot in their own oil.

Lobbyists

Leading the way, **Boeing** reported spending more than $15 million on lobbying in 2013, followed by **Lockheed Martin** ($14.4 million) and **United Technologies Corp**. ($13.6 million). You can believe that these contractors are spending the money to get their greedy paws on some of that just-approved $54 billion.

RID ALL LOBBYISTS FROM WASHINGTON—NOW! These damn political leaders are lining their pockets. Remember: Lawyers know how to make the laws right for themselves. More on this in later chapters.

CHECK THIS OUT!

Hey, big (corporate) spender! Since President Obama took office, General Electric (GE) tops the list. The manufacturing giant has spent around $134 million on lobbying activities since January 2009.

While the reasons vary, it probably has a lot to do with taxes. The company famously paid zero taxes to the U.S. government in 2010 by using a series of deductions to report a $408 million loss in America, even though its international business made a $10.8 billion profit.

Unsurprisingly, defense contractors, including Northrop Grumman (NOC), Boeing (BA) and Lockheed Martin (LMT) are also big spenders on the lobbying front, with the three firms, combined, shelling out almost $280 million since 2009.

The Full List

Here are the publicly-traded companies that have spent the most on direct lobbying since 2009, plus bonuses:

1. General Electric (GE): $134 million
2. AT&T: (T, Tech30) $91.2 million
3. Boeing Co (BA): $90.3 million (defense)
4. Northrop Grumman (NOC): $87.9 million (defense)
5. Comcast Corp (CMCSA): $86.4 million
6. Verizon Communications: (VZ, Tech30) $86.4 million
7. Fed-Ex Corp (FDX): $85.7 million (more coming in another chapter)
8. Exxon Mobil (XOM): $85 million
9. Lockheed Martin (LMT): $78.8 million (defense)
10. Pfizer (PFE): $77.8 million (pill pushers)
16. Google (GOOG): $62.2 million

On December 12, 2016, through his preferred medium, Twitter, president-elect Donald Trump asserted that the unit cost for the fighter jet F-35 was "out of control." On December 19, 2016, U.S. Air Force Lt. Gen.

Chris Bogdan, in charge of the Joint Strike Fighter project, offered his version of things to the press.

The General said each one of the Air Force's F-35A's would cost $102.1 million, while both the U.S. Marine Corps' F-35Bs and U.S. Navy's F-35Cs would set the taxpayer back $132 million each. Those costs average out to approximately $122 million for a "generic" F-35.

Bogdan drew these numbers from the funds Congress had set aside in the 2015 defense budget for what the Pentagon called "Lot 9." Just one of a number of planned F-35 purchases. In November 2016, the U.S. military was still negotiating the final deal with plane-maker Lockheed Martin.

Needless to say, the unit costs Bogdan gave the media were incomplete. They involved only the Pentagon's existing contracts with Lockheed and engine-maker Pratt & Whitney to build the airframes and jet motors.

The numbers do not, for example, include the cost of buying maintenance equipment and other necessary support elements. They do not include money the Pentagon will spend to fix design errors discovered in testing, now and in the future.

The helmet the pilot wears to fly this F-35 runs right at the Million Dollar mark. That is an expensive hat.

Back when I was in the USAF, an F-104 was put into action for $1.42 million. In 55 years, the cost of one aircraft has gone up 100 million dollars. Somebody is making a ton of money. NEGOTIATE.

As of April 15, 2016, the total U.S. cost of the war against the Islamic State in **Iraq** and **Syria** is $7.2 billion, according to a Pentagon estimate. That amount accounts for 617 days of military spending on a war we haven't really gained any ground on.

THE AIR WAR AGAINST ISIS IS COSTING THE U.S. ABOUT $11 MILLION A DAY. I WANT RESULTS! HOW ABOUT YOU?

As of April 4, 2016, the U.S., alone, has conducted 8,584 air strikes since operations began, 5,137 in Iraq and 3,447 in Syria. ISIS is still killing hundreds of men, women and children every month throughout the world.

WHO'S AT FAULT

**Look at UK Manchester, England, where some ISIS nut blew up
and killed over twenty and wounded close to one hundred.
HOW ABOUT SHUTTING OFF ISIS's SUPPLY LINE.
WITHOUT FOOD, WATER AND ARMAMENTS, THEY WILL
FOLD. How many times do I have to say: "SHUT OFF THEIR
SUPPLY LINES.**

With our technology and surveillance equipment, we should be able to shut them down within months. War puts money in the pockets of those who order the items to supply our troops. Money becomes more important than the loss of lives and crippled GIs. THIS WAR GAME HAS BEEN GOING ON FAR TOO LONG. Where the Hell is a Patton-like General to blow these bastards to bits? Patton shut off the Germans' supply line, thus crippling them. When money talks, people die, come home crippled and tax dollars are wasted and there are no wins. Trump is sending 10,000 troops to Iraq and Syria to fight ISIS on the ground. There better not be any ISIS troops left breathing. We better have whipped their asses before I finish this book.

1 million desk jobs

For the first time, the Defense Business Board study was able to count exactly how many people were working in core business operations for the Defense Department. The study divided them into six categories.

Note: Figures are rounded.

Source: Defense Business Board

THE WASHINGTON POST

Approximately **23,000** military and civilian employees and about **3,000** non-defense support personnel work in the Pentagon. It has **five** sides, **five** floors above ground, two basement levels and **five** ring corridors per floor, with a total of **17.5** mi (28.2 km) of corridors. Is everyone productive? Are they carrying their own weight? Is waste overflowing in the 17.5 miles of corridors?

If you believe our United States Defense Department is out of control, then get off your butt and write to your Congressman or U.S. Senator. Remember, if our government stops all wars tomorrow, then many people who currently have cushy jobs in the Pentagon will be out of work. Get a real job. We have way too many government employees.

What Are the Requirements to join the U.S. Military?

Just so you know who really is protecting us here at home. Some men and women join the U.S. military to serve their country and to work at a job that provides a steady income. Others sign up for the opportunity to travel the world. Each of the four major military branches has qualification requirements in areas such as height and weight, age and academics. You can work to meet some of the requirements while still in high school.

Navy

You can join the Navy as an enlisted member or officer. To join as an enlisted member, you must be between the ages of 17 and 34. However, if 17, your parents must consent. United States citizenship or permanent resident alien status is required. If you do not have a high school diploma, a general equivalency diploma is acceptable. The minimum Armed Services Vocational Aptitude Battery, or ASVAB, score to join the Navy is 35. Additionally, before you join the Navy, you must pass at least two drug tests. To become a Navy officer, you must generally be at least 19 and not older than 35. Only United States citizens are allowed to join the Navy as officers. Regarding education, you must possess at least a bachelor's degree before becoming a Navy officer. To enter the officer program, you must also pass two drug tests. Both enlisted and officer members must meet height, weight and physical and mental health standards and complete basic training, which lasts approximately nine to ten weeks.

Army

In addition to being a United States citizen or permanent resident alien, you must have a high school diploma or GED to join the Army as an enlisted member. You must also meet height, weight and overall physical health standards. The minimum score you can get on the ASVAB test is a 31. You have three hours to complete the test, which covers science, math, electronics and reading comprehension. You can become a commissioned officer in the Army if you are a United States citizen. You must also be between the ages of 18 and 35, have at least a bachelor's degree from an accredited postsecondary school and complete a 12-week training program to join through Officer Candidate School, or OCS. Furthermore, you can join the ROTC on a four-year scholarship if you are between 17 and 26 years old. The minimum high school GPA allowed is 2.5. You must score no lower than a 920 on your SAT and at least 19 on your ACT.

Air Force

If you are a United States citizen or legal, permanent resident, you may be able to join the Air Force as an enlisted member. You must be between 17 and 27. If you don't have a high school diploma, a GED is accepted, if you have at least 15 college credits. If you have a high school diploma, you must score at least a 36 on the ASVAB or if you have a GED, you must score at least a 65. Additionally, you must meet height, weight and physical standards. After you pass the ASVAB and physical examinations, you must complete basic training, a rigorous eight-week field and classroom training program. **NOTHING COMPARED TO WHEN I ENLISTED**. You can generally become an Air Force officer by joining and graduating from the Air Force ROTC. In addition to being a United States citizen, you must be between 18 and 34. To join the ROTC, you must be a high school graduate and maintain at least a 2.0 GPA while in college. If you receive an ROTC scholarship, you must maintain at least a 2.5 GPA while in college. As a scholarship recipient, you must complete at least four years of service in the Air Force after graduating college.

Marine Corps

Candidates for the Marine Corps enlisted ranks must be U.S. citizens or legal residents between 17 and 28 years old and have a high school diploma. You must also meet physical requirements and take and pass the ASVAB test with a minimum score of 32. In addition, you must complete and graduate from the 12-week basic training program at Parris Island, South Carolina or San Diego, California. To become a Marine Corps officer, you cannot be younger than 20 or older than 28. In addition to being a United States citizen, officers must have, at the minimum, a bachelor's degree. After you meet height, weight and other physical requirements, you must attend the 12-week OCS, where you will complete classroom courses and physical regimens, including 15-mile endurance hikes.

WITH ALL OF THE ABOVE INFORMATION, I WANT TO KNOW WHY WE CAN'T BEAT THE TAR OUT OF ISIS BEFORE THE END OF 2017. HOW ABOUT YOU? WHAT ARE YOUR THOUGHTS?
TWENTY-THREE PERCENT OF ALL MEN AND WOMEN IN THE U.S. WHO ARE OF AGE TO ENLIST IN ANY BRANCH OF SERVICE CANNOT DUE TO OBESITY AND LACK OF ADEQUATE SCHOOLING. PITIFUL! DISGUSTING! SHAMEFUL AND OUTRAGEOUS.

Chapter 2

UNITED STATES POST OFFICE

The United States Post Office is an absolute disgrace. The United States Postal Service's financial troubles have been well-publicized in recent years. The worst of it came in 2012, when the USPS lost a whopping $15.9 billion dollars, followed by $4.8 billion and $5.3 billion in 2013 and 2014, respectively. There were also large deficits in the range of 5 billion dollars in 2015 and 2016.

Tax breaks

The Post Office is exempt from state and local property and real estate taxes, along with other burdens, such as tolls, vehicle registration fees and parking tickets. These exemptions save the USPS $2.18 billion per year.

Are you kidding me? Where the hell is that savings going?

Cheap borrowing

The Postal Service "can borrow from the U.S. Treasury through the Federal Financing Bank at highly-subsidized interest rates." It currently borrows the legal limit of $15.2 billion at a rate of 1.2 percent. Without this access, it would be paying somewhere between $415 million and $490 million per year more in interest.

USPS is a critical part of the nation's communication and commerce, delivering 154 billion pieces of mail in fiscal year 2015 to approximately 155 million delivery points. The Post Office employs 618,000 people—more than any civilian employer, except Wal Mart. Given the pay and benefit disparities offered by Post Office and private employers, Post Office employees would be highly motivated to block any significant change to the current system. The postman who delivers our mail is the poorest excuse of any postal worker I have ever seen.

A new report profiling the U.S. Postal Service's tenuous financial situation finds it "unlikely" that the government body "will be able to fully make its required retiree health and pension payments in the near future," and its mounting debts and liabilities could threaten its existence and taxpayers' wallets going forward.

WHO'S AT FAULT

In fact, the GAO or Government Accountability Office, found that the USPS only paid $6.7 billion of the $12.6 billion in retiree health and pension payments that were due in fiscal 2015. In last year's 10-K report, the service cited "declines in mail volume" and "statutory and regulatory restrictions" as reasons for defaulting on billions of dollars due to a USPS retiree health benefits fund. The balance came from the US Government Treasury Department—TAXPAYER MONEY.

At the end of fiscal year 2015, USPS had about $125 billion in unfunded liabilities and debt, most of which were for retiree health and pension benefits. These unfunded liabilities and debt are a large and growing financial burden, increasing from 99 percent of USPS revenues in fiscal year 2007 to 182 percent of revenues in fiscal year 2015. What the hell is being done about this problem? Our lazy, absent-minded political leaders in Washington are sitting on their asses without a clue on what to do. So, what else is new?

First-Class Mail has declined 37 percent in volume since peaking in 2001. That volume is expected to continue to decline five to six percent every year going forward, said the GAO.

By the Numbers

68.8 billion — 2015 operating revenue

154.2 billion — number of pieces processed and delivered

47 — percent of the world's mail volume handled by the Postal Service

1.8 billion — dollar amount paid every two weeks in salaries and benefits

493,381 — number of career employees

131,732 — number of non-career employees

31,606 — number of Postal Service-managed retail offices

214,933 — number of vehicles — one of the largest civilian fleets in the world

37 million — number of address changes processed

19.2 billion — total retail revenue

919.5 million — total number of retail customer visits

45.7 — percent of retail revenue from alternative access channels

1.5 billion — total number of visits to usps.com

276.8 million — total Postal Store revenue on usps.com

53.4 million — number of inquiries handled by the Postal Customer Care Center

53.6 million — number of Click-N-Ship labels printed

WHO'S AT FAULT

555.3 million — total revenue, in dollars, from Click-N-Ship label purchases
93 million — number of money orders issued
5.4 million — number of passport applications the Postal Service accepted at post offices
462.8 million — amount in revenue from 2,500 postal Self-Service Kiosks, in dollars
1.1 million — number of new delivery points added to the network in 2015
155 million — total number of delivery points nationwide

Average Starting Pay for Post Office Jobs is $20/hour. U.S. Postal Service jobs offer many fantastic benefits, including: 401K; Free Health Care; Federal Retirement Benefits; Paid Vacation.
FOR HOW LONG IS THE REAL QUESTION.
HOW ABOUT DELIVERY ONLY 5 DAYS PER WEEK? MAYBE PRIVATIZE USPS.
We moved from a condo to an apartment while our new home was being constructed. The area where our new home was being built has two main delivery places on the property. The property manager said we could use the mail box assigned to us and were given keys to our box. After having mail delivered to our new address for two months, the mail carrier informed us since we were not living in our new home yet, we couldn't receive mail in our box. I marched down to the local post office and told the assistant postmaster about my problem. She informed me that I could be a drug pusher and they (USPS) are only allowed to deliver mail where a person is living. We had to fill out new address change forms. Then for the next six months, we only received first class mail. I marched down to the post office and asked to speak to the POSTMASTER. He informed me that I should not be bothering him with such trivial matters. He also informed me that since our current address was only temporary only first-class mail will be delivered. THE DAMN USPS makes a lot of money on second and third-class mail. He informed me the second and third-class mail for my address had been discarded after they charged the sender.

While attending Northern Illinois University back in the late 1960s, I worked four and five mornings per week delivering mail in a small,

WHO'S AT FAULT

residential city, Sandwich, Illinois, reporting to work at 7:00 a.m. I was a substitute mail carrier covering for the other five carriers, who were all receiving maximum vacation and sick time. My postmaster was the best boss I have ever worked for. I almost made a career working for the USPS. My first class at Northern started at 3:00 pm and classes ended at 9:00 pm. Long days back then, especially when I had to drive 45 miles each way.

We have a serious problem when it comes to our USPS. Write your Congressman or U.S. Senator. It is not that the Feds aren't trying to crack down on USPS drug deliveries. According to official U.S. Postal Inspection Service statistics, inspectors seized more than 46,000 pounds of illegal drugs and $20.7 million in drug-trafficking proceeds in the mail last year.

HOW MUCH COULD THEY HAVE STOPPED IF A SEARCH WARRANT WEREN'T REQUIRED?

Postal inspectors are required to secure a search warrant based on probable cause before they can inspect any mail or parcels. According to the USPS:

"Our first-class letters and parcels are protected against search and seizure under the Fourth Amendment to the Constitution, and, as such, cannot be opened without a search warrant." BULLSHIT! You want to stop drug trafficking, then allow postal inspectors to open any piece of mail. They need to put the brakes on the Trillion Dollar drug market. Drug pushers aren't stupid. Our U.S. Government is stupid for allowing the drug cartels to kill people every year by the thousands. Our County in Florida has an epidemic of drug users. In the first three months of 2017, Manatee County paramedics administered 450 doses of Narcan, the brand-name version of the opioid given to people who have overdosed on heroin and other drugs. Again, the paramedics are part of the County which is supported by the taxpayers of the County. Stop the drugs before it hits our shores. One particular man from Manatee County has been given the above-mentioned drug 27 different times in the ER in the past two years at taxpayers' expense.

When you drop your package off at the FedEx or UPS store to be mailed, you are putting the property into the possession of a third party and the Supreme Court has ruled that giving your package to a third party "removes any reasonable expectation of privacy." No drugs running through FedEx and UPS, unless they are missed by the inspectors. **WAKE UP WASHINGTON! Get rid of the United States Supreme Court.** More on this later.

The U.S. Postal Service will be seeking bids for its next generation delivery vehicles. The potential $6 billion deal could be one of the biggest fleet purchases ever. **Where is the money coming from? Borrow the money and add to the national debt. Why not!**

Faced with rising maintenance costs for its aging fleet and needing extra cargo space to satisfy the desires of online shoppers, the U.S. Postal Service is asking automakers to bid on a commercial van that would replace the boxy, Long-Life Vehicle and become the backbone of the service's delivery fleet.

It says it picked vendors last summer to build prototypes, which underwent tests last year, 2016, before a contract is awarded in early 2017.

It could be one of the largest fleet purchases ever in the world. According to specifications released to potential bidders January 20, the Postal Service would buy 180,000 vehicles at $25,000 to $35,000 each, valuing the contract at $4.5 billion to $6.3 billion. **LOBBYISTS WERE LINED UP TO PRESENT THEIR SCHEME ON THIS EXPENDITURE. MONEY TALKS.**

Several paragraphs back I mentioned that the USPS lost $5 Billion last year. First-Class Mail has declined 37 percent in volume since it peaked in 2001. That volume is expected to continue to decline 5-to-6 percent every year going forward, said the GAO. I have repeated this for a reason. Who in GOD'S name is going to pay for these new vehicles that have A/C, back up cameras, right side drive, V-6 automatic four speed transmissions with front wheel drive to carry them through the snow, even when it accumulates in Florida. Some of these new vehicles have already been delivered. I saw one today in Saint Petersburg, Florida. Get your pad and pencil out of the desk drawer and write to your Congressman and Senator.

Chapter 3

PRISON PROBLEM

The United States Prison population is the highest in the entire world. Are we proud or what? We have 724 people for every 100,00 persons incarcerated. This figure is rising every year. Half of the world's prison population of about nine million is held in the U.S., China or Russia.

Race/Ethnicity	% of US population	% of U.S. population incarcerated
White (non-Hispanic)	64%	39%
Hispanic	16%	19%
Black	13%	40%

The U.S. has over 2,220,300 people in prisons or jails. The average cost to house a prisoner is approximately $31,000 per year. You do the math. Prisoners are sitting on their asses. Put them all to work.

In 2011, it cost the U.S. taxpayers a whopping $212 billion to house, feed and clothe these criminals. In 2007, it totaled $74 Billion. During Obama's term, the prison population went down, although crime went up. Now, you figure that out. New York State prisoner cost per year reaches over $60,000. What? Do they have granite counter tops with sleep number beds, gourmet food and wide screen TVs? What a joke! The answer given by New York State: The guards require more wages than other prisons in other states.

A whopping 67% of all prisoners return within a year. What the hell did we teach them while they were incarcerated? Absolutely nothing! Cost too much, they say.

Obama pardoned more prisoners than all the other presidents put together. Do I have to repeat this last sentence?

WHO'S AT FAULT

WASHINGTON — Just weeks before leaving office, President Obama issued 78 pardons and commuted the sentences of **153 prisoners**, extending his acts of clemency to a total of 1,324 individuals.

HOW LONG BEFORE OUR LAW ENFORCEMENT GATHERS THEM UP AND WE START ALL OVER?

Death penalty cases are costing taxpayers billions per year. Lawyers are making the money. Let the bastard rot in his or her cell. It is cheaper to feed them, clothe them and care for them, than to leave them on death row, regardless of how long they live. There is currently a probable death row case in Florida as I type this. Hooray! The judge wasted no time. He gave the SOB life without parole. His victim was not only raped, she was left paralyzed and unable to function for the rest of her life. Yes, she was a brilliant student prior to this bastard ruining her life.

I think all prisoners should work for their place to sleep, their food, their medications and their clean underwear. President Trump wants to build a wall, so put the good prisoners on chains and put them to work. Set up tents and use dogs to control them. Dogs are cheaper than human guards. Prisoners can't run with leg irons on. You think I'm brutal, then stay out of prison.

The states of Texas, Oregon, and Missouri all have legislation requiring that inmates work during their time in prison, meaning that many work even without the pittance that is currently given to them. They should be working to pay for their food, lodging and medical care.

Today, 37 states have legalized the contracting of prison labor by private corporations that mount their operations inside state prisons. The list of such companies contains the cream of U.S. corporate society: IBM, Boeing, Motorola, Microsoft, AT&T, Wireless, Texas Instrument, Dell, Compaq, Honeywell, Hewlett-Packard, Nortel, Lucent Technologies, 3Com, Intel, Northern Telecom, TWA, Nordstrom's, Revlon, Macy's, Pierre Cardin, Target Stores and many more. All of these businesses are excited about the economic boom generated by prison labor. Just between 1980 and 1994, profits went up from $392 million to $1.31 billion. Inmates in State penitentiaries generally receive the minimum wage for their work. Nothing wrong with the wages; here is my only concern: These companies have incarcerated men and women working for them for cheap wages to increase the profits of their companies.

STOCKHOLDERS MAKING BIGGER RETURNS. YES. AND HOW ABOUT THE LOBBYISTS WHO GOT THIS ALL STARTED. THE COMPANIES MENTIONED ABOVE ARE NOT PAYING ANY IMPORT TAX. IF THE PRODUCTS WERE MADE OVERSEAS, THEY WOULD.

My suggestion is for the companies to pay the prison, not the inmate, what the minimum wage would be for work done. Then, that money would be used to maintain the prison. This would cut down on federal and state expenditures. Everyone wins, except the prisoner and that is how it should be. Why should a prisoner win anything?

WHEN YOU PAY THE PRISONERS PEANUTS, HE LEAVES THE CELL PISSED OFF, MAD AT THE JUDGE, THE JURY, THE COP WHO ARRESTED HIM AND THE GUARDS IN THE PRISON. SO, NOW THE GOVERNMENT THINKS HE IS READY TO STEP OUT INTO SOCIETY. WRONG! THIS GUY WANTS TO GET EVEN. SIX MONTHS OR LESS HE IS BACK IN JAIL.

The only education this prisoner gets while incarcerated is from other cell mates. He learns how to get rich without getting caught. What the hell is wrong with giving some needed counseling to get his or her head screwed on straight? Prior to their term in prison, he or she damn sure didn't get any counseling from the parent sitting on the porch. Does our government do anything? What the hell happened to common sense?

The vast majority of working inmates are employed in support roles within the prison: washing dishes, doing laundry, delivering mail, to mention a few. The wages for these jobs are a fraction of what similar work would earn them outside of prison. In the Federal prison system, for example, the pay range is between $0.12 and $0.40 per hour. A few states do not require prisoners to be paid at all. That is also okay. A prisoner should earn his or her right to receive any type of compensation.

WHO'S AT FAULT

Private-run prisons are cheaper to maintain than Federal or State prisons. Big reason: The amount of help is cut drastically.

Statistics from the U.S. Department of Justice show that, as of 2013, there were 133,000 State and Federal prisoners housed in privately-owned prisons in the U.S., constituting 8.4% of the overall U.S. prison population. Broken down to prison type, 19.1% of the Federal prison population in the United States is housed in private prisons and 6.8% of the U.S. State prison population is housed in private prisons. While 2013 represents a slight decline in private prison population over 2012, the overall trend over the past decade has been a slow increase. Companies operating such facilities include the Corrections Corporation of America (CCA), the GEO Group, Inc. (formerly known as Wackenhut Securities), Management and Training Corporation (MTC), and Community Education Centers. In the past two decades CCA has seen its profits increase by more than 500 percent. The prison industry, as a whole, took in over $5 billion in revenue in 2011.

According to some business journalists, Wall Street banks took notice of this influx of cash and are now some of the prison industry's biggest investors. Wells Fargo has around $100 million invested in GEO Group and $6 million in CCA. Other major investors include Bank of America, Fidelity Investments, General Electric and The Vanguard Group. CCA's share price went from a dollar in 2000 to $34.34 in 2013. Sociologist John L. Campbell and activist and journalist, Chris Hedges, assert that prisons in the United States have become a "lucrative and hugely profitable" business.

In June 2013, students at Columbia University discovered that the institution owned $8 million worth of CCA stock. Less than a year later, liberal students formed a group called Columbia Prison Divest and delivered a letter to the president of the University demanding total divestment from CCA and full disclosure of future investments made. By June 2015, the Board of Trustees at Columbia University voted to divest from the private prison industry. Are you kidding me?

Stock prices for CCA and GEO Group surged following Donald Trump's victory in the 2016 election. On February 23, 2017, the DOJ, under Attorney General Jeff Sessions, overturned the ban on using private prisons. According to Sessions, "the (Obama administration) memorandum changed long-standing policy and practice and impaired the Bureau's ability to meet the future needs of the federal correctional system. Therefore, I direct the Bureau to return to its previous approach."

Marijuana Law enforcement cost States an estimated $3.6 Billion per year.

SO, WE LEGALIZE MARIJUANA IN SEVERAL STATES FOR MEDICAL REASONS. WHAT A FREAKING JOKE. WE HAVEN'T ENOUGH PHARMACY DRUGS TO CHOOSE FROM? MY STATE, FLORIDA, JUST VOTED IT IN IN THE LAST ELECTION. MONEY TALKS AND WE, THE PEOPLE, PAY FOR THE MISTAKES MADE BY OUR POLITICAL LEADERS. CALL THEM, WRITE TO THEM, YELL AT THEM ABOUT SOME OF THESE STUPID LAWS THEY INITIATE, OR STAND BY AND WATCH. IT IS TIME TO GET TOUGH. ARE YOU TOUGH ENOUGH?

I have more on decreasing the prison population in my next chapter.

Chapter 4

FAILING EDUCATION SYSTEM

Education spending in the United States for K-12 averaged **$10,700** per pupil (per year) in 2013, according to the U.S. Census Bureau, but that average masked a wide variation, ranging from **$6,555 per pupil** in Utah to **$19,818** in New York.

Over 1.2 million students drop out of high school in the United States every year. That's one student every 26 seconds or 7,000 a day. This is more than alarming!

Some of you may say: "Well, if they drop out, then $10,700 is saved per child." Hey, it would cost over $30,000 per year for that student to be imprisoned. Most dropouts lead themselves to prison within months or a few years after leaving school.

1. About 25% of high school freshmen fail to graduate from high school on time. Alarming!
2. The U.S., which HAD some of the highest graduation rates of any developed country, now ranks 22nd out of 27 developed countries in the world. You should be writing your Senator now. Where is your pen?
3. The dropout rate has fallen 3% from 1990 to 2010 (12.1% to 7.4%). WHOOPY!
4. The percentage of graduating Latino students has significantly increased. In 2010, 71.4% received their diploma vs. 61.4% in 2006. However, Asian-American and white students are still far more likely to graduate than Latino & African-American students.
5. A high school dropout will earn $200,000 less than a high school graduate over his lifetime. And, almost a million dollars less than a college graduate. Yet, they complain about only making ten bucks per hour.
6. In 2010, 38 States had higher graduation rates. Vermont had the highest rate, with 91.4% and Nevada had the lowest, with 57.8% of students graduating.

7. Almost 2,000 high schools across the U.S. graduate less than 60% of their students. Shocking! These neighborhoods are crime-infested, as well. Wake up!
8. These "dropout factories" account for over 50% of the students who leave school every year.
9. One in six students attend a dropout factory. One in three minority students (32%) attend a dropout factory, compared to 8% of white students.
10. In the U.S., high school dropouts commit approximately 75% of the crimes. Are we seeing a pattern here? Is it not the time to write to your Senator and Congressman? The U.S. Supreme Court should have an education plan on their agenda ASAP.

Top Spenders Among States and "State-equivalents," the Census Bureau's Term for D.C.

1. New York ($19,818 per student)
2. Alaska ($18,175)
3. District of Columbia ($17,953)
4. New Jersey ($17,572)
5. Connecticut ($16,631)

Bottom Spenders Among States

1. Utah ($6,555)
2. Idaho ($6,791)
3. Arizona ($7,208)
4. Oklahoma ($7,672)
5. Mississippi ($8,130)

What country spends the most on education per student? Switzerland's total spending per student was $14,922, while Mexico averaged $2,993 in 2010. The average Organization for Economic Cooperation and Development nation spent $9,313 per young person. According to the survey, as a share of its economy, the **United States** spent more than the average country. Yet, we rank 22nd out of the 27 top nations in the world.

WHO'S AT FAULT?
MAKING EVERYONE EQUAL INSTEAD OF SLOTTING STUDENTS ACCORDING TO ACADEMIC LEVEL. DUMBEST THING OUR NATIONAL EDUCATION FOLKS PUT INTO PLAY.

Higher Education

As anyone with a college-age child knows, the cost of sending a son or daughter to a college or university has risen far more than the rate of inflation over the past 10 years. Tuition, fees, room and board and other costs to attend a public or private four-year college have more than doubled.

The average tuition and fees for a private university from 1995 to 2015 jumped 179 percent. Out-of-state tuition and fees at public universities rose 226 percent. In-state national universities rose 296 percent, but is still cheaper than out of state universities.

Last fiscal year, the Florida Lottery rung up **$3.9 billion** in sales. Nearly 60 percent went to the prize pools, seven percent to vendor fees and commissions, and just below two percent to administrative costs, including advertising. That left almost 32 percent—$1.24 billion—for education. YET, we spent all that money and rank 29th in this nation. Something is wrong. Are they stoking the rich kids' schools and giving the poor kids' schools whatever is left over? ABSOLUTELY CORRECT! When Florida started the lottery back in 1986, all money was to go towards education. How would you like to teach in any State's poor neighborhood school where the crime is out of control? More often than not, the parents of these students in poor neighborhood schools are sitting on the porch with their EBT card drinking Pepsi or Coke. Until our government takes control of the waste, this problem will only increase each year. No one should be allowed a FREE RIDE, if capable of working. Get these people off the porch. How in the HELL can the teachers inspire a child whose parents or parent is home collecting? The kid has a very slim chance of completing his high school education and if he or she doesn't then, at taxpayers' expense

($30,000 plus per year), the child will become an adult in prison. Don't forget the taxpayer cost to send an inmate through the court system. We had a young black man in our city here in Florida who was sent to prison for the 22nd time and he is only 35. How's your blood pressure?

Access to a free, quality education is the key to the uniquely American promise of equal opportunity for all.

This promise was formally extended to children with disabilities with the passage in 1975 of landmark Federal legislation now known as the Individuals with Disabilities Education Act (IDEA). Public schools across the country today serve more than six million youngsters with a wide array of disabling conditions. The promise made in 1975 remains unfulfilled.

Ever since its initial enactment, the Federal law has included a commitment to pay 40 percent of the average per student cost for every special education student. The current average per student cost is $7,552 and the average cost per special education student is an additional $9,369 per student, or $16,921. Yet, in 2004, the Federal government provided local school districts with just under 20 percent of its commitment, rather than the 40 percent specified by the law, creating a $10.6 billion shortfall for states and local school districts.

WHERE THE HELL DID THE MONEY GO? Your political leaders turn their heads and bend toward the lobbyists' demands. Get your pen and paper out of the desk drawer.

This shortfall creates a burden on local communities and denies full opportunity to all students—with or without disabilities.

The United States continues to perform below-average in math and middle-of-the-road in reading and science when compared with other industrialized nations.

Schools Meeting Adequate Yearly Progress (AYP) Requirements in 2010-11 Compiled by Center on Education Policy

Schools not meeting AYP requirements	43,738
Schools meeting AYP requirements	46,957
Total Schools	90,695
Did not meet AYP	48%

WHO'S AT FAULT

This number has climbed slightly in recent years. Many years ago, some high schools in this nation of ours had vocational courses for students not college bound. This program has dwindled as some outstanding educators and psychologists came up with the idea all students should be treated equal—all students should have the same curriculum. If we test a student in grade school and he or she doesn't measure up to be a college candidate, then do not try and make him or her a candidate. It will never happen. Money and time wasted on the child resulting in him or her dropping out of school and struggling to survive on the streets. Start training these students to become typists, clerks, plumbers, beauticians, electricians, carpenters, welders, truck drivers, etc., etc. This country has a shortage of all these categories, forcing companies to reach out to hard-working Mexicans to get the job done. If we send all the illegal Mexicans back home tomorrow, this country will fold up in a month.

We just had a new home built in Florida and over 90 percent of the people building the house were Mexicans. Why? Because they will work eight to ten-hour days and show up every day for work. White people and black people won't work in the hot sun, day after day. I know, some do, but the majority do not. The ones that don't want to work, go on welfare and some start dealing in drugs.

Our STUPID GOVERNMENT dishes out EBT cards to those who don't want to work. WHY? THERE ARE HELP WANTED SIGNS POSTED IN MANY BUSINESSES THROUGHOUT MY COMMUNITY, YET OUR POLITICAL LEADERS DON'T WANT MO AND LOLA TO GO HUNGRY. GET A DAMN JOB!

Our fine government lets people (mostly drop outs) stay at home with an EBT card, sitting on the front porch watching the world go by, drinking COCA COLA, while the rest of us are supporting these LAZY GOOD-FOR-NOTHING PEOPLE. **YES, COKE AND PEPSI ARE ALLOWED ON THE EBT CARD.** Coke and Pepsi are in the top twenty in spending money on lobbyists in Washington. Coke and Pepsi are the two biggest products used on EBT cards in America. Obesity, diabetes, etc. are leading causes of poor health for those sitting on the porch. Almost forgot to mention all the sweet treats; such as, Twinkies, cookies, donuts etc., which can be purchased with an EBT card. And, our government keeps on paying them with tax money the rest of us have donated.

NOW DO YOU THINK IT IS TIME TO WRITE YOUR CONGRESSMAN OR SENATOR? ARE YOU FED UP YET? OUR FEDERAL GOVERNMENT IS SPENDING OVER $2.3 BILLION PER YEAR ON FOOD STAMPS. REMEMBER THESE PORCH PEOPLE PRODUCE MORE PORCH PEOPLE OR INCARCERATED PEOPLE THAT THE REST OF US SUPPORT. I KNOW, I'LL HAVE THE PROTESTERS TRYING TO BURN MY HOUSE DOWN.
ENERGY DRINKS CHANGED THEIR LABELS FROM SUPPLEMENTAL TO NUTRITIONAL IN ORDER TO HAVE EBT CARDS PAY FOR THEIR PRODUCTS. THIS WAS DONE WITH LOBBYISTS PAYING OUT TENS OF THOUSANDS OF DOLLARS.
THERE IS OVER $750 MILLION IN EBT FRAUD PER YEAR. EBT CARD CARRIERS ARE SELLING EBT CARDS TO OTHERS FOR CASH, USUALLY TO BUY DRUGS, CIGARETTES, TATTOOS, NAIL POLISH, OR ALCOHOL, JUST TO MENTION A FEW. WITH LESS THAN A HIGH SCHOOL EDUCATION, THESE PEOPLE ARE SMART ENOUGH TO CHEAT AND MANY GET AWAY WITH IT. IF YOU'RE NOT ANGRY BY NOW, THEN NO WONDER THIS COUNTRY IS HEADED FOR DISASTER.

Chapter 5

IMMIGRATION

Before 1965, immigrants coming to American shores had been primarily European. The legislation, also called the Hart-Celler Act, ended the former system of placing quotas on immigrants by national origin; instead, prioritizing skilled workers and family members.

In 1965, 84 percent of Americans were non-Hispanic whites, 12.5 percent Black, 4 percent were Hispanic and less than 1 percent were Asian. In 2015, the numbers are astonishingly different: 62 percent of Americans were white, 14 percent were Black,18 percent were Hispanic and Asians counted as 6 percent of the populace. Our country currently has 1,963,000 Arabs residing in our cities after the 2015 census. Thousands more have filtered into our cities since then.

According to the Pew Research Center, one in five immigrants in the world reside in the United States today. Those immigrants and their children have contributed an estimated 55 percent to the country's population growth during that time; the U.S. population currently stands at almost 322 million. By 2065, nearly 20 percent of people in the country will have been born outside of American borders.

Nearly 59 million immigrants have entered the United States in the last five decades, pushing the nation's foreign-born population close to record highs.

If current trends continue, in the next 50 years the U.S. will be host to 78 million immigrants and immigrants and their descendants are projected to account for 88 percent of the U.S. population increase, or 103 million people.

Nationally, and in many States, the income of immigrant families is not very different from that of non-immigrant families, although individual earnings are lower for immigrants overall. This is because there are typically more workers per immigrant family.

Although most immigrants are not poor, nationally 20 percent live below the poverty line, compared with 16 percent of native-born citizens. Immigrants are also coming in faster, with net international migration adding a new person to the population every 29 seconds (up from one every 33 seconds last year and one every 40 seconds a few years back.)

A total of 38,901 Muslim refugees entered the U.S. in fiscal year 2016, making up almost half (46 percent) of the nearly 85,000 refugees who entered the country legally during that period, according to a Pew Research Center analysis of data from the State Department's Refugee Processing Center. That means the U.S. has admitted the highest number of Muslim refugees of any year since data on self-reported religious affiliations first became publicly available in 2002. Remember, this was Obama's last year in office.

I attended an Air Force reunion last year (2016) in San Antonio, Texas. We took a tour of Lackland Air Force Base and we were informed by a female Air Force sergeant, our tour guide, that thousands of Muslims who had just come to the U.S. were being housed, fed and educated about U.S. culture, rights, money, etc. at the base. All of this paid for with taxpayer money.

Each year the United States sets a numerical limit on how many refugees will be admitted for humanitarian reasons. To be admitted as refugees, individuals must be screened by multiple international and U.S. agencies and prove that they have a "well-founded fear of persecution based on race, religion, membership in a particular social group, political opinion, or national origin." Asylum seekers are individuals already in the United States who fear returning to their home countries. They must prove they meet the definition of a refugee. An immigrant does not qualify as a refugee or for asylum because of poverty or difficult economic conditions in their home country. There are limited forms of temporary humanitarian protection available, but these are rare.

If a person who wishes to immigrate to the United States does not qualify under the family, employment, or humanitarian systems, there may be one other legal path. The annual Diversity Visa program makes 55,000 green cards available to persons from countries with low rates of immigration to the United States. People from Mexico, China, the Philippines, India and other countries with higher levels of immigration to the United States are not eligible. To qualify, applicants must have a high school education and two years of job experience. Since millions of people around the world apply each year, the chances of obtaining a visa through the lottery are extremely low, unless they have help from some of our senators or congressmen.

A look at where refugees to the U.S. have come from and their number provides a glimpse into global events and the U.S.'s role in providing a safe haven. Of the 84,995 refugees admitted to the United States in fiscal year 2016, the largest numbers came from the Democratic Republic of Congo, Syria, Burma (Myanmar) and Iraq.

More recently, the ongoing conflict in Syria has displaced six-in-ten Syrians, or 12.5 million, from their homes, according to a Pew Research Center Analysis of Global Refugee Data. In fiscal 2016, the Obama administration resettled 12,587 Syrian refugees to the U.S., more than 20% above the original target.

HAVE YOU HAD ENOUGH? IF NOT, WHY NOT?

Chapter 6

STUDENT DEBT

It is 2017 and Americans are more burdened by student loan debt than ever before.

You have probably heard the statistics: Americans owe over $1.3 trillion in student loan debt, spread out among approximately 44 million borrowers. In fact, the average Class of 2016 graduate has $37,172 in student loan debt, up six percent from last year. That is with low interest rates. If interest rates go up, the student loans will become harder to pay off. Many more delinquents will appear.

$1.31 trillion in total U.S. student loan debt
44.2 million Americans with student loan debt
Student loan delinquency rate of 11.2%
Average monthly student loan payment (for borrower aged 20 to 30 years): $351
Minimum monthly student loan payment (for borrower aged 20 to 30 years): $203

Loans in repayment borrowers	$478.6 billion	15.7 million
Loans in deferment borrowers	$107.3 billion	3.5 million
Loans in forbearance borrowers	$96.2 billion	2.6 million
Loans in default borrowers	$67.5 billion	4.0 million
Loans in grace period borrowers	$50.1 billion	2.0 million

Combined undergraduate and graduate debt by degree:
Master of Business Administration = $42,000 (11% of graduate degrees)

WHO'S AT FAULT

> Master of Education = $50,879 (16% of graduate degrees)
> Master of Science = $50,400 (18% of graduate degrees)
> Master of Arts = $58,539 (8% of graduate degrees)
> Law = $140,616 (4% of graduate degrees)
> Medicine and health sciences = $161,772 (5%)

To refinance these loans, the interest rates run from 4.23% to 8.24%, depending on credit score.

Approximately 40 percent of the $1 trillion student loan debt was used to finance graduate and professional degrees.

After the student graduates and locates a job, he or she now has the burden of the debt, along with daily living expenses; including, perhaps, the cost of raising a family. It may take ten years to free himself of the student loan debt. Remember, this cuts into the spending he or she may have put towards items that keep this nation running. Debt slows the economy.

STRESS IS RUNNING RAMPANT IN OUR YOUNG, COLLEGE GRADUATES. BRING ON THE MEDS FROM BIG PHARMACEUTICAL COMPANIES TO CONTROL THE STRESS.

What is really troubling to the student who racks up this huge debt is trying to secure a good job in a stagnant market. These students are left with humungous debt, while their college professors are making between $80,000 and $100,000 per year and associates, who do most of the teaching, making $40,000 plus.

How about the college coaches making millions, with TV paying millions to the colleges and giving a FREE ride to student athletes who have an extremely low graduation rate? Is this out of control or what? Check out the college basketball tournament and how many games are televised.

Listed below is the payout to colleges for football.

2014 College Bowl Games	Per Team Pay-Out
CFP Championship	$22,000,000

WHO'S AT FAULT

Sugar Bowl - CFP Playoff Game	$18,000,000
Rose Bowl - CFP Playoff Game	$18,000,000
Fiesta Bowl	$18,000,000
Orange Bowl	$18,000,000
Citrus	$4,250,000
Chick-fil-A Bowl Peach	$3,967,500 (ACC) $2,932,500 (SEC)
Alamo Bowl	$3,825,000
Cotton Bowl	$3,625,000
Outback Bowl	$3,500,000
Ticket City Cactus	$3,325,000
Texas Bowl	$3,000,000
Holiday Bowl	$2,825,000
Music City Bowl	$2,750,000
TaxSlayer (Previously Gator Bowl)	$2,750,000
Russell Athletic Bowl	$2,275,000
Sun Bowl	$2,150,000
Foster Farms	$2,212,500
Pinstripe Bowl	$2,000,000
Belk Bowl	$1,700,000
Liberty Bowl	$1,437,500
Las Vegas Bowl	$1,350,000
Independence Bowl (Duck Commander Bowl)	$1,200,000

Quick Lane Bowl	$1,200,000
Zaxby's Heart of Dallas Bowl	$1,100,000
Military Bowl	$1,000,000
Miami Beach	$1,000,000
GoDaddy.com Bowl	$750,000
Armed Forces	$675,000
Hawaii Bowl	$650,000
Poinsettia	$612,500
St. Petersburg	$537,500
New Orleans	$500,000
New Mexico	$456,250
Bahamas	$450,000
Boca Raton	$400,000
Famous Idaho Potato Bowl	$325,000
Camellia	$100,000

College Basketball Revenue

This year the ACC had six teams in the big dance, which means the Conference is assured $1.5 million this year and another $8 million over the next five just from this year's tournament—and that's assuming all of those teams lose their first-round games. If just one team makes a run to the Final Four, it will add another $1.1 million to the conference take in each of the next six years.

Where does this money go? These figures are in millions.
$205
Sport Sponsorship and Scholarship Funds

Distributed to Division I schools to help fund NCAA sports and provide scholarships for college athletes.

$205

Division I Basketball Fund

Distributed to Division I conferences and independent schools based on their performance in the men's basketball tournament over a six-year period.

$94.3

Division I Championships

Includes support for team travel, food and lodging.

$79.9

Student Assistance Fund

Distributed to Division I student-athletes for essential needs that arise during their time in college.

$73.7

Student-Athlete Services

Includes funding for catastrophic injury insurance, drug testing, student-athlete leadership programs, postgraduate scholarships and additional Association-wide championships support.

$3

Educational Programs

Supports various educational services for members, including the Women Coaches Academy, the Emerging Leaders Seminars and the Pathway Program.

There are eight additional places they send money to: None of them are to help the student debt problem. What a money-maker for the colleges.

The 65 universities that comprise the Power Five conferences (plus Notre Dame) totaled $6.3 billion in **revenue** during 2014-15. Last year marked the debut of the **College Football** Playoff, restructured bowl contracts that were far more lucrative and the start of the SEC Network. The gap in **revenue** can be startling.

College Football Reaches Record $3.4 Billion in revenue and college students are squeezed by over a trillion dollars in student loans. Does this need to be corrected?

WHO'S AT FAULT

College coaches are making millions to support a Billion Dollar business. If they are fired, they still get what remains on their contract. It is all about winning and nothing else. Must win a football game, but losing a war is okay. I used to be a sports nut, especially college basketball, pro-baseball and pro-football. Not anymore, except for pro-baseball. It is out of control in most sports.

Chapter 7

INFRASTRUCTURE

The American Society of Civil Engineers says the U.S. needs massive investments in all essential **infrastructure**, from bridges and airports to dams and railways. According to the society's most recent **infrastructure** report card, the U.S. earns a D+ for its **infrastructure**. It is, in a word, a huge mess.

Areas include

Infrastructure on the National Register of Historic Places
Infrastructure in the United States by State
Infrastructure in American Samoa
Infrastructure in Guam
Infrastructure in Puerto Rico
Infrastructure in the United States Minor Outlying Islands
Infrastructure in the United States Virgin Islands

Dams in the United States
Energy infrastructure in the United States
Flood control infrastructure in the United States
Mines in the United States

Nuclear weapons infrastructure of the United States
Proposed infrastructure in the United States
Public services of the United States
Sewerage infrastructure in the United States
Transportation infrastructure in the United States
Water supply infrastructure in the United States

Highway Funding

Unfortunately, highway fund revenues have been insufficient to fully fund existing highway spending, with Congress authorizing billions of dollars in transfers from the U.S. Treasury's General Fund into the Highway Trust Fund to keep it solvent, including a $10.8 billion transfer in August 2016. It has ongoing funding needs that will continue unless a more permanent solution can be found, either by raising the national gas tax (which hasn't been increased since 1993), or some other funding measure. The Congressional Budget Office expects the Highway Trust Fund to have an annual shortfall of $15 billion.

A number of solutions have been proposed, including mileage-based fees on drivers, additional gas taxes, or simply pulling more money from the Treasury's General Fund. And that's *just* for highways. Wait and see is the usual answer coming out of Washington for damn near everything. Meanwhile, the problem accelerates until something catastrophic happens.

Falling Down Bridges

One in ten bridges is deemed structurally deficient, meaning the bridge has a significant defect that requires reduced weight or speed limits. (It does not necessarily mean the bridge is unsafe.) Another 14 percent of the nation's 607,380 bridges are considered "functionally obsolete," meaning they are no longer suited to their current task because of overuse or a lack of safety features, yet are still in use.

Waterways

Inland waterways, including canals and rivers, move the equivalent of 51 million truckloads of goods every year—and half the locks are more than 50 years old. According to the ASCE (American Society of Civil Engineers), the problem is so bad that many barge operators have supported an increase in their fuel tax to increase funding to the Inland Waterways Trust Fund, the main user funding mechanism for construction and rehabilitation of inland waterways. So, what needs to be done?

Ports, Harbors, and Dams

Then, there are the hundreds of commercial ports and harbors. But it is not the cargo terminals that need upgrading—they have seen significant investment as shipments in standardized containers have risen over the past couple of decades. Instead, it is the navigation channels that need upgrading and taxpayers foot that bill.

Our dams are equally in need of investment and upgrades. In 2012, nearly 14,000 dams were considered a high-hazard, where failure of the dam would likely cause the loss of life. They're not necessarily unsafe, OR ARE THEY? But if they were to fail, very bad things would result. The nation's 84,000 dams are owned and operated by the Federal Government; the rest are managed by State governments, regional authorities or private entities, such as utility companies.

AGAIN, OUR ABSENT-MINDED POLITICIANS IN WASHINGTON AND AT THE STATE LEVEL, AS WELL, ARE JUST SITTING THERE COLLECTING A PAYCHECK, WHILE OUR INFRASTRUCTURE IS FALLING APART. LOBBYISTS DON'T GET INVOLVED IN INFRASTRUCTURE UNTIL THE MONEY IS ACTUALLY ALLOCATED TO BE USED FOR SUCH.

That leads us to what really forged this country ahead—the Railroads. They, too, are in dire need of repair, especially the bridges. I recently visited Europe and used the Euro-rail on various occasions. Fantastic system, to say the least.

GET YOUR PEN OUT AND WRITE YOUR POLITICAL LEADERS A LETTER NOW TO GET THEM OFF THEIR BUTTS TO GET SOMETHING DONE BEFORE OUR COUNTRY HAS A CATASTROPHIC ACCIDENT DUE TO POOR INFRASTRUCTURE.

President Trump wants $1 trillion to get the infrastructure program started. The cronies you elected will lolly-gag around for months, only to decide to put it off and continue to feed the people sitting on the porch more junk food. Politicians will help voters long before they will help our nation. Votes get them elected, so they can reap the kickbacks paid out by the large companies.

WHO'S AT FAULT

WAKE UP PEOPLE. UNLESS YOU WRITE TO YOUR LEADERS, THEY WON'T BUDGE AN INCH. THEY DON'T WANT TO LOSE YOUR VOTE.

Chapter 8

MEDICAL INSURANCE

National health expenditures will hit $3.35 trillion this year, which works out to $10,345 for every man, woman and child. OUT OF SIGHT!!

Of the total $3.35 trillion spending projected this year, hospital care accounts for the largest share, about 32 percent. Doctors and other clinicians account for nearly 20 percent. Prescription drugs bought through pharmacies account for about 10 percent. The balance of 38% is for administrative, maintenance and miscellaneous.

U.S. health care spending is wildly uneven. About five percent of the population—those most frail or ill and poor—account for nearly half of the spending in a given year. The poor can be controlled. Let's get on it.

How many people in the U.S. are obese? More than two-thirds (**68.8** percent) of adults are considered to be overweight or slightly obese. More than one-third (**35.7** percent) of adults are considered to be obese. More than 1 in 20 (6.3 percent) have extreme obesity. Almost three in four men (74 percent) are considered to be overweight or obese. I think the figures above are on the low side if you just look at what is standing in line at the grocery stores. Take notice of what is in their cart.

The medical care costs in the United States associated with obesity are high. In **2008 dollars**, these costs were estimated to be **$147 billion**. The annual, nationwide, productive costs of obesity-related absenteeism range between $3.38 billion ($79 per obese individual) and $6.38 billion ($132 per obese individual).

REMEMBER THE PEOPLE SITTING ON THE PORCH DRINKING PEPSI AND COKE EATING TWINKIES AND SWALLOWING ENERGY DRINKS. LOBBYISTS ARE SUCKING UP THE MONEY, WHILE WE, THE HARD-WORKING TAXPAYERS, ARE PAYING FOR THE OBESITY. WHAT DOES OBESITY COST AMERICA? THE ESTIMATED ANNUAL HEALTH CARE COSTS OF OBESITY-RELATED ILLNESSES ARE A STAGGERING $190.2 BILLION OR NEARLY 21 PERCENT OF ANNUAL MEDICAL SPENDING IN THE

UNITED STATES. CHILDHOOD OBESITY ALONE IS RESPONSIBLE FOR A WHOPPING $14 BILLION IN DIRECT MEDICAL COSTS.

In addition, obesity is associated with job absenteeism, costing **approximately $4.3 billion** annually. Lower productivity while at work costs employers $506 per obese worker per year.

But, there are tens of thousands who are not sitting on the porch and are either working or retired and suffer from diabetes. Yes, I'm being hard on overweight people. My mother, a registered nurse, whom I loved dearly, died of diabetes due to being overweight. No excuses for most.

AS A PANEL OF SCIENTISTS CONSIDERS WAYS TO HELP AMERICANS TRIM DOWN, WIDESPREAD OBESITY RAISED MEDICAL-CARE COSTS BY $315.8 BILLION IN 2010. HAVE YOU SEEN ANY PHYSICAL FITNESS PROGRAMS BEING PROMOTED BY OUR POLITICAL LEADERS?

By Mayo Clinic Staff

Obesity usually results from a combination of causes and contributing factors, including:

Genetics

Your genes may affect the amount of body fat you store, and where that fat is distributed. Genetics may also play a role in how efficiently your body converts food into energy and how your body burns calories during exercise.

Family lifestyle

Obesity tends to run in families. If one or both of your parents are obese, your risk of being obese is increased. That is not just because of genetics. Family members tend to share similar eating and activity habits.

Inactivity

If you are not very active, you don't burn as many calories. With a sedentary lifestyle, you can easily take in more calories every day than you burn through exercise and routine daily activities.

Unhealthy diet

WHO'S AT FAULT

A diet that's high in calories, lacking in fruits and vegetables, full of fast food, and laden with high-calorie beverages and oversized portions contributes to weight gain.

Medical problems

In some people, obesity can be traced to a medical cause, such as Prader-Willi syndrome, Cushing's syndrome and other conditions. Medical problems, such as arthritis, also can lead to decreased activity, which may result in weight gain.

Certain medications

Some medications can lead to weight gain if you don't compensate through diet or activity. These medications include some antidepressants, anti-seizure medications, diabetes medications, antipsychotic medications, steroids and beta blockers.

Social and economic issues

Research has linked social and economic factors to obesity. Avoiding obesity is difficult if you don't have safe areas to exercise. Similarly, you may not have been taught healthy ways of cooking, or you may not have money to buy healthier foods. In addition, the people you spend time with may influence your weight—you're more likely to become obese if you have obese friends or relatives.

Age

Obesity can occur at any age, even in young children. But as you age, hormonal changes and a less active lifestyle increase your risk of obesity. In addition, the amount of muscle in your body tends to decrease with age. This lower muscle mass leads to a decrease in metabolism. These changes also reduce calorie needs and can make it harder to keep off excess weight. If you don't consciously control what you eat and become more physically active as you age, you will likely gain weight.

Pregnancy

During pregnancy, a woman's weight necessarily increases. Some women find this weight difficult to lose after the baby is born. This weight gain may contribute to the development of obesity in women.

Quitting smoking

Quitting smoking is often associated with weight gain. And for some, it can lead to enough weight gain that the person becomes obese. In the long run, however, quitting smoking is still a greater benefit to your health than continuing to smoke.

WHO'S AT FAULT

Lack of sleep

Not getting enough sleep or getting too much sleep can cause changes in hormones that increase your appetite. You may also crave foods high in calories and carbohydrates, which can contribute to weight gain.

IF OUR POLITICAL LEADERS WOULD GET OFF THEIR ASSES AND PASS A BILL TO SHRINK THE OBESITY PROBLEM IN THE U.S., IT WOULD, PERHAPS, SLOW THE WEIGHT PROBLEM DOWN. HOW ABOUT TAKING FAT FOOD OFF EBT CARD CARRIERS? OUR COUNTRY IS OUT OF SHAPE. THE POLITICAL LEADERS MUST DO SOMETHING IMMEDIATELY OR THIS COUNTRY IS NOT ONLY GOING TO GO BROKE FROM WASTEFUL SPENDING, BUT WILL BE SWALLOWED UP IN TOO MUCH BLUBBER.

As of 1962, about 46 percent of adults in the United States fell into the categories of overweight, obese, and extremely obese. About 32 percent of adults were overweight, about 13 percent were obese and about 1 percent had extreme obesity. In other words, this country has gotten FAT and LAZY and, now, we are in a very serious situation.

HOW ABOUT PHYSICAL FITNESS FOR ALL AMERICANS, WHETHER SHORT, TALL, FAT, OR THIN, OLD OR YOUNG. WE HAD SUCH A PROGRAM YEARS AGO. WERE YOU ON IT OR WERE YOU TOO LAZY TO PARTICIPATE?

Around 10.6 million Americans have been left broke by insurance premiums, co-pays and doctor's bills. WHY? Hospitals, pharmaceutical companies and doctors are ripping Americans off. Pharmaceutical companies have some of the largest groups of lobbyists in Washington. They spend millions every year just to keep screwing the public for their Damn pills. Political leaders in Washington could care less about your drug costs per year. They get FREE medical and FREE medications.

I am old enough to use VIAGRA. Try buying Viagra at your local Pharmacy—$40.00 per pill. INSANE! Imagine a guy on a tight, fixed income? Beer or Viagra? Buying and using Viagra is like paying for sex.

WHO'S AT FAULT

Drug manufacturers in the U.S. set their own prices. That is not the norm elsewhere in the world. The FDA takes a long time to approve generic drugs. We allow "government-protected monopolies" for certain drugs, preventing generics from coming to market to reduce prices. Sometimes, State laws and other "well-intentioned" Federal policies limit generics' abilities to keep costs down. Drug prices aren't really justified by Research and Development.

And, this is a serious problem because drug prices decline to 55 percent of their original brand name cost once there are two generics on the market and to 33 percent of original cost with five generics.

Pharmacists in 26 states are required by law to get patient consent before switching to a generic drug. This reportedly cost Medicaid $19.8 million dollars in 2006 for just one drug: a statin called simvastatin, whose brand name is Zocor. Costs ran higher because pharmacists didn't get patient consent and Medicaid had to pay for the costlier brand-name drug, even though a cheaper product was available. **THIS IS WRONG!**

In 2010, prescription drug expenses were ten percent of the $2.6 trillion of total health-care spending in the United States, making it the third largest services portion of healthcare expenditure, followed only by hospital, physician and clinical spending.

There is no doubt too many people are taking too many pills per day. Who is pushing them down their throats? You guessed it— DOCTORS. But not all doctors. My doctor doesn't.

EAT RIGHT AND GET SOME EXERCISE

The *Washington Post* wrote in 2003 that "U.S. Customs estimated ten million U.S. citizens brought in medications at land borders each year. An additional two million packages of pharmaceuticals arrive annually by international mail from Thailand, India, South Africa and other points." Prescription drugs also entered the country in large quantities through Canada, because of the price differential of prescription drugs in the two countries. In 2004, it was estimated that Americans purchased more than one billion U.S. dollars in brand-name drugs per year from Canadian pharmacies to save money.

Drug manufacturers may offer to pay an insurance company a rebate after selling them a drug for full price. This is largely invisible to the consumer, because a drug company does not report how much money it returns to the payer. In 2012, the aggregate in the U.S. has been estimated at $40 billion per year. How much are they giving these damn insurance companies today? Why the hell aren't our political leaders putting a stop to this payout. Reason: They (political leaders) are saddled up with the pharmaceutical and insurance lobbyists. They have large smiles on their faces as we, the taxpayers, suffer.

In 1992, the Prescription Drug User Fee Act (PDUFA) was passed, making it the law for pharmaceutical companies to directly pay the FDA to review their applications for drug approvals. That way, the FDA has more resources to conduct rigorous and timely reviews, pharma companies get products through the regulatory pipeline faster and patients get new drugs more quickly. Win-win-win, right?

Reports found that since PDUFA was passed, pharma companies have contributed **$7.67 billion** to the federal agency. **WHERE THE HELL IS THAT MONEY GOING?**

Illegal Immigrants

These are the "squatters" of American society. They enjoy the privileges—and many of the benefits—earned by those who reside here legally: Protection from harm, emergency medical care, and public education. Their children, if born in the U.S., receive automatic citizenship. According to the National Research Council, the cost to the American taxpayers of 11 million illegal aliens is estimated at $346 billion annually.

Medical costs specifically for uninsured illegal individuals are estimated at $4.3 billion per year, according to the Center for Immigration Studies, primarily due to the use of emergency rooms and free clinics. This does not include the billions of dollars more that are being absorbed by hospitals for inpatient care.

PRESIDENT TRUMP BETTER DO SOMETHING QUICK. OUT OF CONTROL!

Chapter 9

LOBBYISTS

How much does a lobbyist make a year? As of November 7, 2016, a Lobbyist earned a median annual salary of **$105,881**, with a range between **$85,229** to **$146,156**. However, this can vary widely depending on a variety of factors.

Lobbying (also **Persuasion**) is the act of attempting to influence the actions, policies, or decisions of officials in their daily life, most often legislators or members of regulatory agencies. Lobbying is done by many types of people, associations and organized groups, including individuals in the private sector, corporations, fellow legislators or government officials, or advocacy groups (interest groups). The term "lobbying" appeared in print as early as 1820.

There are about 16,000 lobbyists registered at the Federal level. That means there are about 20 plus lobbyists for every member of the House of Representatives and U.S. Senate. Let us not forget about the State you live in. Oh, yes, they have lobbyists as well, who rip off the taxpayers daily.

Together, they spend more than $3 billion every year trying to influence members of Congress, according to the Center for Responsive Politics in Washington, D.C.

At the Federal level, a lobbyist is defined by the law as someone who earns at least $3,000 over three months from lobbying activities, has more than one contact he is seeking to influence and spends more than 20 percent of his time lobbying for a single client over a three-month period.

Critics say the Federal regulations are not strict enough and point out that many former lawmakers perform the functions of a lobbyist, but don't actually follow the same pattern.

How Can You Spot a Lobbyist?

At the federal level, lobbyists and lobbying firms are required to register with the Secretary of the U.S. Senate and the Clerk of the U.S. House of Representatives within 45 days of making official contact with the President of the United States, Vice President, member of Congress or certain Federal officials.

The list of registered lobbyists is a matter of public record. Lobbyists are required to disclose their activities of trying to persuade officials or influence policy decisions at the Federal level. They are required to disclose the issues and legislation they are attempting to influence, among other details of their activities.

IN PUBLIC OPINION POLLS, LOBBYISTS RANK SOMEWHERE BETWEEN SEWAGE WATER AND NUCLEAR WASTE. IN EVERY ELECTION, POLITICIANS VOW NEVER TO BE "BOUGHT OUT" BY LOBBYISTS, BUT OFTEN ARE. TOO DAMN OFTEN!

As of 2015, more than 16,000 Federal lobbyists were registered under the Lobbying Disclosure Act. You have to be kidding me!

On March 24th, 2017, the House Republicans pulled the Medical Insurance Bill to replace Obamacare because they did not have enough votes to carry the bill to the Senate if the vote had taken place. Lobbyists are the winners, along with the Representatives. Now, millions of people in our country will suffer for months because our existing Medical Insurance Program sucks. Do these people have any regard for the human race?

I BELIEVE STRONGLY THAT ALL LOBBYISTS SHOULD BE REMOVED FROM WASHINGTON AND NEVER ALLOWED TO PRACTICE THEIR LOBBYING ANYWHERE IN THE UNITED STATES. DO I NEED TO REPEAT THIS LAST SENTENCE?

The Top Lobbying Industries in The United States and What They Spend on Lobbying in Washington, DC

Industry	Total
Pharmaceuticals/Health Products	$3,515,091,778
Insurance	$2,420,777,769

Industry	Total
Electric Utilities	$2,183,268,654
Business Associations	$2,015,257,992
Electronics Mfg. & Equip	$2,006,622,646
Oil & Gas	$1,900,998,075
Misc. Manufacturing & Distributing	$1,552,500,796
Education	$1,514,194,951
Hospitals/Nursing Homes	$1,450,514,056
Telecom Services	$1,410,117,480
Securities & Investment	$1,407,011,840
Real Estate	$1,365,525,210
Civil Servants/Public Officials	$1,328,514,989
Health Professionals	$1,312,333,848
Air Transport	$1,251,399,940
Misc. Issues	$999,713,055
Defense Aerospace	$994,671,141
Automotive	$984,213,735
Health Services/HMOs	$983,256,640
TV/Movies/Music	$942,648,229

DID YOU HAPPEN TO NOTICE THE AMOUNT OF MONEY SPENT ON HEALTH CARE? NOW YOU KNOW WHY THE NEW HEALTH CARE BILL DIDN'T GET PASSED.

As companies became more politically active and comfortable during the late 1980s and the 1990s, their lobbyists became more politically visionary. For example, pharmaceutical companies had long opposed the idea of government adding a prescription drug benefit to Medicare on the theory that this would give the government bargaining power through bulk purchasing, thereby reducing drug industry profits. But, sometime around 2000, industry lobbyists dreamed up the bold idea of proposing and supporting what became Medicare Part D—a prescription drug benefit, but one which explicitly forbade bulk purchasing—an estimated $205 billion benefit to companies over a ten-year period. This small amount of money above is one of ten thousand reasons why our country is $20 Trillion in the red.

IN MY OPINION, THE ABOVE IS STEALING. STEALING IS A CRIME. CRIMINALS SHOULD BE INCARCERATED. IF YOU OR I WERE INVOLVED IN THIS CRIMINAL ACT, WE WOULD BE IN PRISON.

Lobbyists have the right to lobby. This is protected by both the First Amendment and the Lobbying Disclosure Act of 1995 and, additionally, by the inherent need for participation in our democratic environment. Lobbying is an integral part of a modern participatory government and is legally protected. What a bunch of bull crap that is.

Over 50 percent of all members of Congress are millionaires. Over 65 percent of the members of the U.S. Senate are millionaires. Less than 60 percent of both houses are lawyers. That shocked me. Only one percent of the U.S. population is classified as a millionaire. So, tell me how can a millionaire in Washington understand what a household making $56,000 (the national average) is going through on a daily basis? A person making less than $100,000 per year could never become a Senator or Congressman. It takes tons of money to even think about it.

I realize President Trump is a multi-billionaire, but he shows me more compassion for the normal U.S. citizen than any President since former President Ronald Reagan. The reason, I believe, is because neither one was a life-long politician before becoming President. Even though President Reagan was Governor of California, I never classified Reagan as a politician. Neither one owed anyone anything when they became President. President Trump draws no salary. Yes, he receives a salary, but donates all of it. He just donated his first three months' salary (over $73,000) to the National Parks Service.

Chapter 10

FOREIGN AID

In fiscal year 2014, the U.S. government allocated the following amounts for foreign aid:

Total military assistance: $10.57 billion
Total economic assistance: $32.53 billion
Total economic and military assistance: $43.10 billion

Foreign aid for fiscal year 2017: $42.3 billion (A decrease, but not enough of a decrease.)

How Was This Aid Distributed?

Clearly, not all aide is distributed equally. The question is: Who received the largest slice of the pie from the U.S.? **Israel**

Of the $32.53 billion of total economic aid distributed, almost a quarter of the funds went to five countries. Below are the top five recipients of economic aid in 2014:

Israel: $3.1 billion
Egypt: $1.5 billion
Afghanistan: $1.1 billion
Jordan: $1.0 billion
Pakistan: $933 million

At first glance, one may wonder why Israel would receive roughly nine percent of U.S. economic aid. It is important to note that foreign aid has a variety of uses depending on the current political, economic, and social climate. According to the U.S. State Government 2013-2015 Foreign Assistance report, all $3.1 billion of Israel's funding was used for military financing. In Egypt, $1.3 billion of the $1.5 billion received was used for military-related activities as well. On the other hand, the majority of funds received by Afghanistan, Jordan, and Pakistan were used for economic development purposes. Of the $35 billion referenced in the report, $8.4 billion (24 percent) was used towards global health programs, $5.9 billion (17 percent) was used for foreign military financing, $4.6 billion (13 percent) was used for economic support, and $2.5 billion (7 percent) was used for development assistance.

Below is a breakout of aide received by geographic region in fiscal year 2014.

Africa: 20 percent
East Asia and Pacific: 2 percent
Europe and Eurasia: 2 percent
Near East: 20 percent
South and Central Asia: 7 percent
Western Hemisphere: 4 percent
General Aid: 45 percent

With 142 countries receiving aid out of the 188 countries listed with the International Monetary Fund (IMF) in 2014, approximately 76 percent of the world received some form of economic assistance from the U.S., the majority located within Africa and the Near East. Depending on future geopolitical events, this allocation is subject to change; however, according to the Federal government's 2015 estimates, the approximate $33 billion requests in aide follow a similar geographic allocation. Nonetheless, in the past three years, the economic support from the U.S. will have impacted a large majority of the world's population, totaling $103 billion in economic support across various programs.

The vast majority of spending on health goes to HIV/AIDS projects. In 2014, the U.S. spent $3.1 billion on HIV/AIDS—about a fifth of the foreign aid budget. The next two big health categories were "Maternal and Child Health," at about $530 million, and malaria, at about $470 million. Of all the global health expenditures, a category labeled "Pandemic Influenza and Other Emerging Threats" receives the least funding, about $66 million in 2014. Funding for the U.S. Ebola response counts as emergency assistance and is not included in the budget.

THE U.S. SPENDS APPROXIMATELY ONE PERCENT OF ITS TOTAL BUDGET ($4 TRILLION IN 2016) ON FOREIGN AID. DOESN'T SEEM LIKE MUCH MONEY, BUT WHEN YOU ARE 20 TRILLION DOLLARS IN DEBT, A THOUSAND DOLLARS BECOMES TOO MUCH.

Mexico received a total of **$769,853** in disbursed aid from the United States government in 2017, a **decrease** of 6,835 percent from the last reported total in 2016 ($53.4 million). It is about time. Look how much Mexico makes on products made in their country that U.S. depends on.

OUR FEDERAL GOVERNMENT SPENDS APPROXIMATELY $80.37 PER YEAR, PER TAXPAYER, ON FIGHTING POVERTY AROUND THE WORLD. WE HAVE TENS OF THOUSANDS LIVING IN POVERTY HERE. HOW ABOUT SPENDING $80.00 ON GETTING THE PORCH-SITTERS OFF THEIR ASSES AND DONATE $.37 TO FOREIGN COUNTRIES TO FIGHT POVERTY. MONEY SAVED IS MONEY EARNED.

Mexico Exports to the United States

1. Vehicles

At over $68.6 billion, vehicles accounted for almost a quarter of all goods coming into the U.S. from Mexico in 2016. This category includes $21.8 billion worth of passenger cars and $20 billion worth of vehicle parts. American auto makers, such as General Motors and Ford, have plants in Mexico. **Let Mexico pay for the WALL.**

2. Electric Machinery

Through November 2016, nearly 21 percent or $57 billion of U.S. imports were smaller electric appliances; such as, phones, televisions, vacuum cleaners and parts. Devices and parts used in telephony ranked the highest in this category, with an $11.8 billion import value, followed by televisions and related parts, valued at $9.7 billion.

3. Optical, Photo, Medical & Surgical Instruments

The $12.2 billion of imports under this category is not just a significant figure, but also an eight percent improvement over the import figure for the same period in 2015. Instruments used in surgeries and medical procedures, at $5.37 billion, were the largest chunk of the total, whereas other instruments made up imports valued at $900 million.

4. Crude Oil

Despite being the one of the largest crude oil producers in the world, U.S. consumption exceeds domestic production. As of November 2016, the crude oil import figure from Mexico stood at $6.9 billion. **WHY?**

5. Fresh Veggies

Mexico is the biggest source of all agricultural imports for the U.S. Last year (2016), the U.S. brought in $5 billion worth of vegetables through November, an increase of a little over four percent as compared to the entire year of 2015. Tomatoes, onions and bell peppers are popular vegetable imports from Mexico.

6. Fresh Fruits

The U.S. imported over $1.5 billion worth of avocados, amounting to nearly a third of the $4.5 billion total fruit import figure through November 2016. This figure was higher than the full-year fruit import total for 2015 by close to 2.2 percent.

7. Wine & Beer

Mexico is famous for its tequila, but the U.S. imported nearly $2.9 billion worth of beer from its neighbor in the first eleven months of 2016, a 3.7 percent increase from the $2.7 billion imported during the entire previous year.

Chapter 11

GOVERNMENT SUBSIDIES

A **subsidy** is a benefit given by the **government** to groups or individuals, usually in the form of a cash payment or a tax reduction. The **subsidy** is typically given to remove some type of burden, and it is often considered to be in the overall interest of the public. Yeah, Right!

"Uncle Sam's Favorite Corporations"

1. Boeing: $13,174,075,797
2. General Motors: $3,494,237,703
3. Royal Dutch Shell: $2,038,202,298
4. Dow Chemical: $41,408,228,374
5. Goldman Sachs: $661,979,222

These five are the top companies receiving the most government subsidies from U.S. taxpayers, which is in addition to their own profits. Over the course of 15 years, the Federal government has distributed $68 billion in grants and special tax credits to businesses, with two thirds of that transferred to large corporations. Six companies have received $1 billion or more, while 21 have received $500 million or more.

Between 2001-2006, farm subsidies tapered off a bit, averaging $19 billion a year. Of this, possibly $15 billion was wasteful, unnecessary or redundant. Between 1995-2010, farm subsidies had ballooned to $52 billion a year, on average. Of this, more than six percent went toward four "junk food" components: corn syrup, high-fructose corn syrup, corn starch and soy oils. Many people wondered why the Federal government was subsidizing food that contributed to America's obesity problem. **Duh!**

Since 1979, the corn industry has received $20 billion in Federal subsidies, recently reaching $6 billion a year. The purpose was to divert production into ethanol, a component of gasoline. The subsidies were to help producers meet a 2005 Federal law that required 7.5 billion gallons of renewable fuel be produced by 2012. In 2007, a revision increased the goal to 36 billion gallons by 2022. Only 6.25 billion gallons were produced in 2011.

WHO'S AT FAULT

The Export Credit Guarantee Program provides commercial financing to enable the exports of U.S. farm products. Specifically, the USDA guarantees the credit of foreign buyers when they can't get credit approval locally.

The Dairy Export Incentive Program (DEIP) pays cash subsidies to dairy exporters to help them meet the subsidized prices of foreign dairy producers.

Housing subsidies promote home ownership and support the home-builder industry. They take two forms: interest rate subsidies and down-payment assistance. The primary interest rate subsidy is the mortgage interest deduction on the Federal income tax. There are also some smaller interest subsidies, such as tax exemptions on municipal bond interest used to subsidize mortgages for low-income families. They total about $15 billion a year.

These direct homeowner subsidies paled in comparison to what the Federal government spent to support its FHA mortgage loan guarantee program. The real trouble started when it created two government-sponsored enterprises, Fannie Mae and Freddie Mac, to provide a secondary market to buy these mortgages from banks. When they bought too many subprime mortgages, the government spent $130 billion to bail out Fannie and Freddie and, eventually, nationalize them. Was the bailout a subsidy? Yes, in a sense, because without it, there would have been no housing activity whatsoever after the subprime mortgage crisis. REALLY! That's because Fannie, Freddie, and the Federal Home Loan Guaranty Corporation were behind 90 percent of all home loans, effectively replacing the private sector's role in the home mortgage market in the U.S.

The U.S. Federal Government offers many more subsidies, which it thinks will improve the economy. For example, the Cash for Clunkers program in 2009 was considered a subsidy to the auto dealer, according to the Bureau of Economic Analysis. In this program, the dealer received a $3,500-$4,500 subsidy from the Federal government after discounting a new vehicle to a consumer who had traded in an old car. The goal was to jump-start the economy after the recession and to encourage people to buy more fuel-efficient vehicles and lessen U.S. reliance on foreign oil.

What a line of Bull Crap is this? All of these subsidies are political give-a-ways. The money used is the taxpayer's money. It is then allocated to companies and businesses who have the leverage to demand the subsidy.

WHO'S AT FAULT

The taxpayer loses again, except for the cash they received for the clunker and that was an absolute joke.

American taxpayers give an $18 billion gift (subsidy) to the post office every year. That figure will rise after their purchase of 180,000 new vehicles in 2017 at $30,000 plus per unit. Get out your calculator. And most of the deliveries to your mail box is junk mail.

I HOPE YOU HAVE READ ENOUGH ALREADY TO WRITE YOUR SENATORS AND CONGRESSMEN AND LET THEM KNOW YOU ARE FED UP WITH THE WASTEFUL SPENDING. IF NOT, THEN KEEP ON READING. YOU ARE ABOUT HALF-FINISHED.

Chapter 12

FREE MEDICAL FOR WHOM?

Medicare was signed into law in 1965. At the time, the House Ways and Means Committee predicted the program would cost $12 billion in 1990. By the time 1990 rolled around, the actual cost was $110 billion. This year, Medicare costs are estimated to hit nearly $600 billion. As if stuck in an infinity loop, Medicare and big paramedical companies (which have successfully manipulated the political system to their advantage) drive health care costs above the stratosphere.

Completely opposite of other countries, American laws actually prevent the government from restraining drug prices. Federal law even prevents the single largest drug buyer– Medicare –from negotiating drug prices. This is a perfect example of how Big Pharma has successfully manipulated laws in such a way that they can operate completely unrestrained in the U.S.—**PITIFUL!**

However, Congress does not control what drug makers charge for their drugs. Pharmaceutical companies are allowed to set their own prices and when it comes to one-of-a-kind drugs, like some cancer drugs, the safeguards built into a free-market system disappear, making price setting anything but fair. Why the hell not? Nobody in Washington is trying to stop them? Remember: The folks in Washington get FREE MEDS and Medical Coverage. **READ THIS LAST SENTENCE AGAIN.**

Pharmaceutical companies also give rebates to hospitals to create an incentive to dispense the drug, as the hospital can then make a greater profit. But, since hospitals around the country not only get the same drug at varying rates and the "average sales price" Medicare bases its payments on doesn't necessarily reflect these rebates, the base price Medicare uses is most often not very average at all. In some cases, this can result in a hospital still making up to a 50 percent profit on what Medicare pays for the drug!

As a result of laws and regulations preventing the U.S. government from reining in drug prices like other nations do, drugs are wildly overpriced in the U.S. Overall, Americans pay *50 percent more* than other countries for identical drugs. This year alone, the U.S. will spend more than $280 billion on prescription drugs. If Americans paid the same prices other countries pay for the same products, we would save about $94 **billion** a year! The explanation given by the pharmaceutical industry when confronted about this price difference is: ***"U.S. profits subsidize the research and development of trailblazing drugs that are developed in the U.S. and then marketed around the world."***

A certain article lists 50 signs that the U.S. health care system is a gigantic money-making scam that is about to collapse. This list includes the following amazing statistics:

This year the American people will spend approximately $2.8 trillion on health care. It is being projected that Americans will spend $4.5 trillion on health care in 2019 unless the program changes from Obamacare to something everyone can afford. Our political leaders are working on it between recesses and the other political BS about Russia running our election and Trump being considered for impeachment by the opposite side due to kissing up to Putin. They should be worried about Obama and Hillary and Bill Clinton's shenanigans with uranium. Hang onto you shorts when this fire starts to really burn.

If the U.S. health care system were a country, it would be the sixth largest economy on the entire planet. **Don't get sick.**

Approximately 60 percent of all personal bankruptcies in United States are related to medical bills. Stay healthy.

Since 1998, the U.S. health care industry has spent more than $5 **billion** on lobbying our politicians in Washington D.C. **CORRUPTION AT ITS FINEST.**

The U.S. ambulance industry makes more money each year than the movie industry. Did that surprise you? The employees inside the vehicle are not making that kind of money.

Another factor driving this broken health care system is direct-to-consumer drug advertising. According to Fierce Pharma, the pharmaceutical industry spent $2.7 billion on TV drug ads, as well as in magazines, newspapers, radio and billboards over the past ten years. I thought it was more than that.

"The world's largest drug company, Pfizer, tops the list, spending 23 percent of that $2.7 billion on some of its best-selling drugs. In fact, as the data show, it is generally a company's best-selling drugs that get the greatest spends, suggesting that DTC, or Depository Trust Company, advertising remains very effective." The

WHO'S AT FAULT

DTC holds trillions of dollars' worth of securities, including corporate bonds, municipal bonds and money market instruments. It settles funds after each trading day using Fed-wire Funds Service.

YOU ALL PROBABLY KNEW THIS ALREADY, BUT I THREW IT IN JUST TO GET YOUR BLOOD PRESSURE UP AND GET YOU TO WRITE YOUR POLITICAL LEADERS IN WASHINGTON.

The U.S. far outpaces every country in **both** raw spending and spending as a percentage of GDP. The U.S. is nowhere near first place for life expectancy (15th out of 34th) or quality of care, despite all that spending. The DTC broke down OECD's, Organization for Economic Co-operation and Development, based in Paris, France, key statistics and found three major reasons why American healthcare costs are so much higher.

Americans spend **160 percent** more on drugs vs. the Netherlands and about **36 percent** more than the next-highest-spending countries (Japan and Canada). That is partly because Americans want a pill for everything, but mostly because the U.S. has generous patent protections for drug makers allowing them to charge high prices.

Hospital costs in the U.S. are the highest in the world at **$10,300** per stay. Hospital costs make up 16 percent of total healthcare costs. In the Netherlands, the average hospital stays costs about **$4,100.** These are primarily administrative costs, which include legal staff and expenses (due to too damn many lawyers ready to sue). U.S. hospitals also have higher-than-average profit margins.

Medical costs specifically for uninsured individuals are estimated at $4.3 billion per year, according to the Center for Immigration Studies, primarily due to the use of emergency rooms and free clinics. This doesn't include the billions of dollars more that are being adsorbed by hospitals for inpatient care.

Why is this happening? This country's beneficence is unmatched. In 1986, when Congress enacted the Emergency Medical Treatment & Labor Act (EMTALA), it ensured public access to all comers for emergency services, regardless of an ability to pay. WHOA! Does it pay to sit on the porch and be poor? I guess so.

Illegal immigrants, who have not paid anything into the Medicaid program at all, are reportedly receiving approximately $2 billion annually in benefits under the Emergency Medicaid program as part of a State-Federal health insurance program for the poor. Look at the money we could save if we left the U.S. and returned as illegal immigrants.

It is obvious why mothers come to birth their babies in the U.S. This is the land of opportunity compared to their native countries. The standard of health care is second to none. With the multiple entitlement programs from birth through K-12, their children have opportunities that never would have been available to them if their mother had not immigrated here. And under the 14th Amendment, children born in this country to undocumented parents are automatically granted citizenship. The numerous entitlement programs for which these infants are eligible are said to generate costs to the United States at a current rate of $58 billion a year. Remember this figure will rise to the moon if we don't stop illegal immigrants from squatting on our soil.

Again, once an illegal woman delivers her baby on U.S. soil, the baby becomes a U.S. citizen. Then, mother and father, if he is available, live here with their U.S. baby. Delivery and care of baby is **FREE. IF IT'S FREE, IT'S FOR ME. WOW!** And we are paying the bill.

WE ARE THE ONLY CIVILIZED NATION IN THE WORLD THAT ALLOWS CITIZENSHIP TO A NEWBORN CHILD. HAVE YOU HAD ENOUGH? READY TO WRITE YOUR CONGRESSMAN AND SENATOR?

Chapter 13

TRANSPORTATION SECURITY ADMINISTRATION

The **TSA** was created as part of the Aviation and Transportation Security Act sponsored by Don Young in the United States House of Representatives and Ernest Hollings in the Senate, passed by the 107th U.S. Congress and signed into law by President George W. Bush on November 19, 2001. It was formed as a response to the September 11, 2001 attacks.

Transportation Security Officers

The TSA employs approximately 47,000 Transportation Security Officers (TSOs), often referred to as screeners or agents. They screen people and property and control entry and exit points in airports. They also observe several areas before and beyond checkpoints. TSOs carry no weapons and are not permitted to use force, nor do they have the power to **arrest.**

Key Requirements for Employment
Be a U.S. Citizen or U.S. National at time of application submission
Pass a credit and criminal check
Be at least 18 years of age at time of application submission
Pass a Drug Screening and Medical Evaluation
No default on $7,500 or more in delinquent debt (except for some bankruptcies)

As of September 2014, the starting salary for a TSO was $25,773 to $38,660 per year, not including locality pay (contiguous 48 states) or cost of living allowance in Hawaii and Alaska. A handful of airports also have a retention bonus of up to 35 percent. This is more than what private screeners were paid.

Transportation Security Inspectors (TSIs)

They inspect and investigate the security of passenger and cargo transportation systems. TSA employs roughly 1,000 aviation inspectors, 450 cargo inspectors and 100 surface inspectors.

National Explosives Detection Canine Teams Program

These trainers prepare dogs and handlers to serve as mobile teams who can quickly find dangerous materials. As of June 2008, the TSA had trained approximately 430 canine teams, with 370 deployed to airports and 56 deployed to mass transit systems.

In 2008, TSA officers began wearing new uniforms that have a blue-gray, 65/35 polyester/cotton blend duty shirt, black pants, a wider black belt, and optional short-sleeved shirts and black vests (for seasonal reasons). The first airport to introduce the new uniforms was Baltimore-Washington International Airport. Starting on September 11, 2008, all TSOs began wearing the new uniform. One stripe on each shoulder board denotes a TSO; two stripes, a Lead TSO; and three, a Supervisory TSO.

For fiscal year 2012, the TSA had a budget of roughly $7.6 billion. Part of the TSA budget comes from a $2.50 per-passenger tax. So, in other words Mr. Taxpayer, they are double dipping every one of us Taxpayers prior to getting on any commercial flight. **Re-read this last sentence.**

As of 2011, the TSA employed about 60,000 screeners in total (including both baggage and passenger screeners). Approximately 500 TSA agents have been fired or suspended for stealing from passenger luggage since the agency's creation in 2001. The airports with the most reported thefts from 2010 to 2014 were JFK (New York), followed by LAX (Los Angeles) and MCO (Orlando). A total of 25,016 thefts were reported over the five-year period from 2010 to 2014. What kind of people are we screening for employment? Probably none of them came off the porch, or did they?

The TSA has also been criticized for not responding properly to theft and failing to reimburse passengers for stolen goods. For example, between 2011 and 2012, passengers at Hartsfield–Jackson Atlanta International Airport reported $300,000 in property lost or damaged by the TSA. The Agency only reimbursed $35,000 of those claims. Similar statistics were found at Jacksonville International Airport—passengers reported $22,000 worth of goods missing or damaged over the course of 15 months. The TSA only reimbursed $800. Now, we know that some people just put in claims to get cash refunds without having lost a single item.

Current List of Acceptable IDs

Drivers' licenses, or other state photo identity cards, issued by Department of Motor Vehicles (or equivalent) in accordance with REAL ID enforcement

U.S. passport

U.S. passport card

DHS trusted traveler cards (Global Entry, NEXUS, SENTRI, FAST)

U.S. military ID (active duty or retired military and their dependents, and DoD civilians)

Permanent resident card

Border crossing card

DHS-designated enhanced driver's license

Airline-or airport-issued ID (if issued under a TSA-approved security plan)

Federally recognized, tribal-issued photo ID

HSPD-12 PIV card

Foreign government-issued passport

Canadian provincial driver's license or Indian and Northern Affairs Canada card

Transportation worker identification credential

Immigration and Naturalization Service Employment Authorization Card

Do you feel safe getting on your favorite airline today? Did you ever just scan the waiting area and see what type of person is riding on your plane? You hope that 70 percent of them don't sit next to you.

The FY2017 President's Budget

The FY2017 Budget of $7.6 billion will allow TSA the opportunity to more fully address the additional requirements identified last year in response to findings from covert testing of screening processes and procedures by the Department of Homeland Security's (DHS) Office of the Inspector General (OIG).

If I were the President of the United States, I would request a study be done on all TSA employees and equipment used to make sure our butts are safe in the sky and the airports.

I believe you could cut the staff by 30 percent without blinking an eye. I have travelled many miles via airlines since 9/11, including 30 days after 9/11, and I have seen a lot of TSA employees scratching their asses, picking their noses, talking to other TSA employees, eyeballing the opposite sex going through the scanner and some even texting while on the clock. In other words, not doing what they are paid to be doing. A disgrace to say the least. Maybe the study would discover the benefits of privatizing TSA. Remember, our Government has more employees than any other corporation in the world. Helps keep unemployment down.

Additionally, Atlanta's airport (TSA employees) has only Black employees. JFK, DC, and Chicago employ mostly Black TSAs. WHY? I have nothing against Black people, but it's not right to discriminate.

The Federal workforce is 17.8 percent Black, 8.1 percent Hispanic, 5.6 percent Asian/Pacific Islander, 1.7 percent Native American, 0.8 percent non-Hispanic/Multi-racial, and 66.0 percent White. Minorities, as a whole, constituted 34.0 percent of the Federal workforce. Men comprised 56.1 percent of all Federal, permanent employees and women, 43.9 percent. Re-read this last paragraph.

THE TRANSPORTATION SECURITY ADMINISTRATION HAS FIRED MORE THAN 1,200 PASSENGER SECURITY SCREENERS AFTER BACKGROUND CHECKS SHOWED THAT SOME OF THEM WERE CONVICTED FELONS.

The above is an absolute joke. Never hire prior to the background check has been completed. This could have been deadly for hundreds of passengers. Is the TSA doing background checks on future employees who are immigrants from Arab countries?

I have talked to several airline pilots and have been informed that cargo, baggage handlers and ramp employees punch a clock prior to working and never pass through any security checks before or after work. WHY NOT? Pilots and stewardesses are screened.

Chapter 14

ENTITLEMENTS

Definition: An individual's right to receive a value or benefit provided by law. **Entitlement Programs** of the Federal Government include Medicaid, Medicare, Social Security, Unemployment and Welfare Programs. Biggest question many people have is why are these called entitlements? We paid into these programs for years. Right?

Total annual spending will increase by **$2.3 trillion** in nominal terms, growing from **$3.5 trillion** in 2014 to $5.8 trillion in 2024. Social Security, Medicare, and Medicaid made up 77 percent, or more than three-fourths, of mandatory program spending in 2014 and have no budget limits.

IF YOU ARE YOUNGER THAN 50 WHILE I'M TYPING THIS, DON'T PLAN ON GETTING YOUR SOCIAL SECURITY ENTITLEMENT. THERE WON'T BE ANYTHING LEFT. OUR FEDERAL GOVERNMENT HAS ROBBED PETER TO PAY PAUL FOR MANY YEARS. SOCIAL SECURITY FUNDS WILL RUN OUT BY 2034—17 MORE YEARS! TOO BAD. YOU PEOPLE UNDER 50 HAD PARENTS WHO ALLOWED THE POLITICAL LEADERS TO BLOW YOUR SO-CALLED ENTITLEMENTS. NOW, YOU SAVE AND SPEND LESS, THUS PUTTING YOUR WONDERFUL COUNTRY INTO A DEEP RECESSION.
OUR STUPID POLITICIANS HAVE USED SOCIAL SECURITY FUNDS ON OTHER GOVERNMENT PROGRAMS. MAINLY, TO CARE FOR THE PORCH PEOPLE MENTIONED EARLIER IN THIS BOOK. THESE POLITICIANS DON'T RECEIVE SOCIAL SECURITY, AS THEY ARE GOVERNMENT EMPLOYEES. BUT YOU CAN BET THE FARM THEY WILL GET FULL RETIREMENT BENEFITS INCLUDING FREE MEDICAL UNTIL SOMEONE THROWS DIRT ON THEIR GRAVE. OOOPS! THEIR SPOUSES WILL GET THEIR RETIREMENT AND FREE MEDICAL CARE UNTIL THE DIRT FILLS THEIR GRAVE. THIS IS WRONG!

WHO'S AT FAULT

A January 12, 2014 Cato Institute Report shows that the Federal government spends **$668 billion** per year on 126 different welfare programs (spending by the State and local governments push that figure up to **$1 trillion** per year). Believe me, that figure hasn't gone down since 2014.

PRESIDENT TRUMP HAS HIS WORK CUT OUT FOR HIM THE NEXT FOUR YEARS. MORE GOING OUT THAN COMING IN ALWAYS PRESENTS A PROBLEM. WE, THE HARD-WORKING CITIZENS, MUST STRUGGLE TO MAKE ENDS MEET, WHILE OUR POLITICAL LEADERS HELP OUT THE PORCH PEOPLE (NINE PERCENT OF THE TOTAL BUDGET IS WELFARE) SO THEY MAKE SURE THEY GET THEIR VOTE AT ELECTION TIME. THIS SCENARIO HAS BEEN GOING ON WAY TOO LONG.

Welfare cost is only two percent higher than the 2017 interest on our National Debt. **OUT OF CONTROL, FOLKS!** What the hell are you going to do about it? Cry in your milk? Stand up and demand that your political leaders cut expenses until the debt is cleared.
STOP ALL IMMIGRANTS (LEGAL OR ILLEGAL, WHICH INCLUDES PREGNANT WOMEN) FROM COMING INTO OUR COUNTRY UNTIL WE GET OUR COUNTRY'S DEBT PAID OFF. THIS COUNTRY CAN'T AFFORD ANYMORE IMMIGRANTS, REGARDLESS OF WHERE THEY COME FROM, UNTIL WE GET OUR DEBT UNDER CONTROL. I WOULD LIKE TO SEE A FIVE-YEAR MORATORIUM ON ANY IMMIGRANTS FROM ENTERING OUR COUNTRY UNTIL WE GET THIS COUNTRY BACK ON ITS FEET.

I Just read in this morning's paper about the State of Oregon wanting to register babies (newborns) as Democrats. Wow! These political people will stop at nothing. I can see it now on Facebook: "My two-day old daughter is a registered Democrat. What a &%#*@ JOKE!

Chapter 15

SECRET SERVICE

Why is it called the Secret Service?
Because it was originally a domestic intelligence and counterintelligence agency. The first one in U.S. history, in fact. Until 2003, the U.S. **Secret Service** was the **Secret Service** Division of the Department of the Treasury. Basically, they were the law enforcement arm of the Treasury Department. The United States Secret Service is now a federal law enforcement agency under the U.S. Department of Homeland Security.

Headquarters: Washington, D.C
Resident agent offices: 68
Number of employees: 6,750
Founded: July 5, 1865, Washington, D.C.
Annual budget: $2.8 billion (2014) WOW!

The Secret Service was created in 1865 to investigate counterfeit money. At the time, it was estimated between one-third and one-half of all money in the U.S. was counterfeit.

In 1894, President Grover Cleveland asked for part-time protection at his vacation home, but it wasn't until after President McKinley was shot in 1901 that the commander-in-chief had full-time protection.

After Robert F. Kennedy's assassination in 1968, Congress authorized protection of "major" presidential and vice-presidential candidates and nominees within 120 days of the general election. According to 18 United States Code #3056, "major" candidates are those identified by the Secretary of Homeland Security and an advisory committee.

Heads of State and their spouses, foreign dignitaries and official representatives of the United States conducting special missions abroad also travel with the Secret Service. Some Cabinet members in the presidential order of succession, U.S. Senators and members of Congress receive protection.

WHO'S AT FAULT

Through an executive order, the President may also designate protection for others. For security reasons, the Secret Service doesn't share specifics. If you were to ask the Secret Service Bureau who gets the protection and who does not, they are not going to tell you.

The Secret Service is also in charge of security for huge special events; such as, presidential inaugurations and national political conventions. The President's (OBAMA'S) Fiscal Year 2016 Budget Request of $41.2 billion for the Department of Homeland Security reflects our continued commitment to ensuring a homeland that it is safe and secure.

IF OUR COUNTRY WERE MORE PARTICULAR ABOUT WHO ENTERED OUR LAND, THE BUDGET WOULD PROBABLY DECLINE. WHAT DO YOU THINK?

Do former Presidents have Secret Service for life?

Life-time, government-provided security for former **Presidents** was the law of the land until 1997, when Congress passed legislation limiting **Secret Service** protection to ten years after leaving office. The 1997 law said any **President** serving before January 1, 1997 would still **receive** the lifelong protection.

With the stroke of a pen, President Barack Obama changed the law and gave himself and his wife Secret Service protection for the rest of their lives.

The new law, which passed the House and Senate in December, 2016, designates that all former U.S. Presidents who served after January 1, 1997, along with their spouses, receive protection from the Secret Service for their entire lifetimes—meaning former President George W. Bush and his wife, Laura, are also covered. The law also stipulates that children of Presidents receive protection until the age of 16.

Salaries

According to the **Secret Service** website, uniformed division officers had a typical starting annual **salary** of about $52,000 in 2010 and special agents were hired at **salaries** ranging from about $44,000 to $75,000.

	Min-Max (in thousands)	Average Per Year
Special Agent **FBI** 34 salaries	$72-$163	$127,641
Special Agent **US Immigration and Customs Enforcement** 30 salaries	$69-$142	$96,338
Special Agent **US Department of Homeland Security** 26 salaries	$67-$160	$123,544

Prospective Secret Service agents must typically
 Possess a bachelor's degree
 Have no visible body markings (tattoos, piercings etc.)
 Go through an extensive interview process
 Successfully complete a strenuous physical fitness exam
 Pass a Treasury Enforcement Agent exam
 Pass a written skills test

Communications

The agency uses Motorola XTS and APX radios and surveillance kits in order to maintain communications. These radios are known to use DES (Data Encryption Standard) encryption keys. When operationally required, members of the Special Operations Division use military grade radios that use Type 1 encryption algorithms.

Vehicles

When transporting the President, the Service uses a fleet of custom-built armored Cadillac Parade Limousines, the newest and largest version of which is known as "The Beast".
How much is the presidential limo worth?

There is no car like the President's armored limo—"The Beast". Designed from the ground up by the Secret Service, President Barack Obama's **$1.5 million** "Cadillac One," is a moving fortress, impenetrable by bullets and bombs. The car is 18 feet in length, weighs eight tons and has eight-inch-thick armor plating on its doors. When the President is riding in one, the vehicle is officially known as Cadillac One. It might surprise you to learn that President Barack Obama's massive Cadillac isn't really a Cadillac. And there is not one, but a dozen, in the highly classified motor pool, each costing more than **$1 million**. I wonder what the lobbyist made off this deal? Barack Obama and his family **cost** the taxpayers $1.4 billion per year. This included paying for hundreds of **Secret Service** agents. And even the Obamas' dog, Bo, cost the taxpayers thousands of dollars. His handler reportedly received over $100,000 a year. I never could find the value of Bo's Pooper Scooper. I understand that the #2 deposits from Bo are immediately destroyed.

When logistics require such a vehicle or when a low-profile appearance is required, armored, Chevrolet Suburbans are used. For official movement, the limousine is affixed with U.S. and Presidential flags, as well as the Presidential seal on the rear doors. For unofficial events, the vehicles are left sterile and unadorned.

Weapons

The current sidearm for USSS agents is the SIG Sauer P229 chambered in .357 SIG, which entered service in 1999 and the FN Five-seven pistol. A variety of off-duty, back-up and undercover weapons are also authorized- Agents and officers are trained on standard shoulder weapons that include the FN P90 submachine gun, the 9mm Heckler & Koch MP5 submachine gun and the 12-gauge Remington 870 shotgun The agency has initiated a procurement process to ultimately replace the MP5 with a 5.56mm rifle.

As a non-lethal option, Special Agents, Special Officers and Uniformed Division Officers are armed with the ASP baton and Uniformed Division officers carry pepper spray.

A new report from the Inspector General of Homeland Security found it took the Secret Service a year to replace a broken

alarm system at former President George H.W. Bush's home. Government jobs always take longer, especially if one party (DEMOCRATS) is getting work done for another party (REPUBLICANS) or vice versa.

Chapter 16

NATIONAL PARKS

The system includes 417 areas, covering more than 84 million acres in every State, the District of Columbia, American Samoa, Guam, Puerto Rico, and the Virgin Islands. These areas include national parks, monuments, battlefields, military parks, historical parks, historic sites, lakeshores, seashores, recreation areas, scenic rivers and trails, and even the White House.

How many employees are in the National Park Service?
Permanent, temporary, and seasonal: Approximately 22,000 diverse professionals
Volunteers in Parks: Nearly 340,000 in 2016

How many people visit the national parks?
Total recreational visitors to the national parks in 2016: 330,971,689. We have more people working or volunteering than we do visitors visiting. Why not, taxpayers are paying for it.

Budget
FY2014 Enacted: $2.98 billion
FY2015 Request: $3.65 billion
FY2015 Enacted: $2.61 billion
FY2016 Request: $3.0 billion
FY2016 Enacted: $2.85 billion
FY2017 Request: $3.1 billion

2016 marked the 100th anniversary, the Centennial year, of the National Park Service, offering a defining moment and an opportunity to reflect and celebrate in preparation for a new century of stewardship and engagement. FY2017 is an opportunity to build on the success of the Centennial and continue the momentum into the second century. The roots of the National Park Service lie in the parks' majestic, often isolated natural wonders, and in places that exemplify America's cultural heritage, but parks and public lands now extend to places difficult to imagine 100 years ago—into urban centers, across rural landscapes, deep within oceans and across night skies.

A Call to Action seeks to chart a path towards a second century vision for the National Park Service by asking employees and partners to commit to concrete actions that advance the mission of the Service within four broad themes.

In support of these efforts, Congress provided $34.9 million in FY2015, including $8 million to restore seasonal capacity, $4 million to expand youth employment programs, $2 million to increase volunteer management capacity, $10.9 million to complete repair and rehabilitation of park facilities and $10 million to support Centennial Challenge projects. In FY2016, Congress provided an additional $122.1 million in support of the Centennial Initiative, including an increase of $89.6 million to address the deferred maintenance backlog through line item construction, repair and rehabilitation, and cyclic maintenance projects, as well as another $8 million to support seasonal rangers, $2 million more for volunteer management capacity, $17.5 million to support new parks and critical responsibilities, including $1.5 million for landscape restoration at new park areas and an additional $5 million for Centennial Challenge projects. The FY2017 request builds on the funding previously provided, particularly the funding to address the deferred maintenance backlog on the NPS' highest priority, non-transportation assets. The President's request includes a discretionary increase of $190.5 million to invest in the second century of the NPS. This includes discretionary increases of $150.5 million in operations and construction, which coupled with a mandatory proposal discussed below, will allow the NPS to restore and maintain all 7,186 highest priority non-transportation assets in good condition over the next ten years. The other increases for operations would support the "Every Kid in a Park Initiative," including $11.5 million to transport more than one million students from Title 1 elementary schools in urban areas to nearby national parks and $8.5 million to support park-level youth engagement coordinators. Additionally, the request includes an increase of $20 million for Centennial Challenge projects and partnerships, a matching program which would leverage federal funds with partner donations for signature projects and programs at national parks.

In September 2015, the Administration proposed the National Park Service Centennial Act, which included several mandatory funding proposals. This included $100 million a year for three years to provide the federal match for Centennial Challenge projects, as well as $300 million a year for three years to support Second Century Infrastructure Investment projects that address deferred maintenance. Finally, the proposal included the NPS Second Century Fund, which would provide the authority for the NPS to collect additional camping and lodging fees, as well as funds collected from purchases of the lifetime pass for citizens age 62 years or older, in order to complete projects and programs in support of the NPS mission; funds would be matched by partner donations of cash, goods or services. The impact of this new revenue source is estimated at $40.4 million in 2017, including $37.6 million from fees and pass sales.

The National Park Service (NPS) receives annual appropriations in the Interior, Environment and Related Agencies appropriations bill. For FY2017, the Obama Administration requested $3.101 billion in discretionary appropriations for NPS, an increase of 8.8 percent over the enacted FY2016 amount. THE NPS estimates that funding in FY2017 would support a total of 20,486 full time equivalents, of which 16,713 would be funded from discretionary authority. In addition to the discretionary funding, the Obama Administration proposed $1.238 billion in mandatory appropriations for NPS, a growth of 135.6 percent over NPS mandatory funding in FY2016. Parts of the mandatory request would require changes in authorizing law. The discretionary and mandatory requests brought the Obama Administration's total request for NPS for FY2017 to $4.339 billion, a requested increase of 28.5 percent over the FY2016 total.

Historic Preservation Fund

This appropriation, which supports Historic Preservation Offices in states, territories, and tribal lands for the preservation of historically and culturally significant sites, is proposed to be funded at $87.4 million in FY2017, an increase of $22 million over the FY2016 enacted level. Of the $25.7 million requested across the budget for a Cultural Resource Challenge, the HPF account includes increases of $2 million to support grants to tribes, $3 million to support grants to historically Black Colleges and Universities and $17 million to support competitive grants for the sites and stories of Civil Rights in America. The increases proposed for grants to HBCUs, as well as the competitive grants, are also part of the Civil Rights Initiative which seeks to preserve, document, and interpret the stories of the Civil Rights Movement and the African-American experience.

ARE YOU READY TO WRITE YOUR CONGRESSMAN AND SENATOR? I HOPE SO! NOW WE ARE RELOCATING OR TEARING DOWN CIVIL WAR STATUES.

More than $1.2 million in Yosemite Conservancy grants since 1998 have funded a variety of bear-management tools for the park, including the creation of the new website. Conservancy support has also gone to improving monitoring and tracking technologies, purchasing and installing thousands of bear-proof food lockers for campers and funding research and educational programs. As a result of the programs, the number of annual bear-related incidents in the park have been reduced significantly. Incidents dropped from 1,584 in 1998 to fewer than 100 in 2016.

Yosemite National Park is home to between 300 and 500 American black bears.

The Park Service maintains a park construction priority list. Buildings in Yosemite need a new electrical system to protect visitors from electrocution and fire. Without a new sprinkler system, Park officials say, a fire could destroy Independence Hall in thirty minutes. Members of Congress and, in particular, members of the Appropriations Committees, routinely ignore these priorities by bumping home district projects up the list. Senator Dale Bumpers, a member of the Appropriations Committee, made sure that the Park Service spent $12 million restoring a row of abandoned bathhouses in Hot Springs Park. This was only number 110 on the Park Service's priority list; 60 items that were ahead of it on the list didn't get funded at all. Depends on who blows enough smoke.

Meanwhile, parks like Yosemite and Yellowstone lack funds for basic maintenance and upkeep. Yosemite is not getting $5 million to repair an electrical system that the Park Service said posed "severe safety" problems for visitors. In Yellowstone, 90 percent of the trails and 80 percent of the roads need repairs.

WHO'S AT FAULT

The majority of park construction and maintenance costs go for visitor centers, employee housing, and whatever is left goes towards roads. The Park Service seems to have some unwritten rules about these facilities:

1. Nearly every park seems to need a multimillion-dollar Visitors Center. Why so much? Maybe there's a Lobbyist involved.

2. Nearly every rural park seems to need extravagant employee housing.

3. Most expensive of all, nearly every park needs roads costing a million dollars or more per mile.

Responding to Congress' preference for pork barrel construction, the Park Service spends lavishly on these facilities. A typical visitors center covers 7,500 square feet—as much as four, three-bedroom houses. Before recent timber price increases, construction costs alone averaged $300 to $350 per square foot—three times the cost of normal office construction. When water, sewer, landscaping, parking lots and furnishings were added, total costs typically approached $8 million. The Park Service commonly plans such visitor centers for parks that receive more than 100,000 visitors per year.

Employee housing is also expensive. The Park Service has 4,700 housing units—bunkhouses, apartments, or individual homes—for employees in rural parks. Employees pay rent, averaging about $200 per month, which is dedicated to maintenance. However, the rent fails to come close to covering all of the costs. As a result, the Park Service says that it needs well over $500 million to repair, rehabilitate, or replace existing housing, an average of over $110,000 per unit.

HAVE YOU EVER SEEN SO MANY FIGURES IN THE MILLIONS OF DOLLARS? DISGUSTING! HOW ABOUT USING PRISONERS AS THE LABOR FORCE?

Every time the Federal Government gets their fingers into any kind of budget they, without any doubt, blow the money on something stupid. The things that need to be addressed go without, thus costing millions of dollars more to replace or refurbish at a later date. That is why we need more business-minded people in Washington. Remember that the next election. I have said it for years. We need to vote out the majority of the lawyers out of Washington, now. In a recent edition of my local paper, a

WHO'S AT FAULT

resident wrote an article in the Letter to the Editor section. He stated that our U.S. government is not a business. The government should not be interested in balancing a budget. I totally disagree. When you are talking about trillions of dollars, then our government is one humungous business.

Chapter 17

FREE GOVERNMENT HOUSING

Section 8 of the Housing Act of 1937 (42 U.S.C. § 1437f), often called **Section 8**, as repeatedly amended, authorizes the payment of rental housing assistance to private landlords on behalf of approximately 4.8 million low-income households, as of 2008, in the United States. The largest part of the Section is the Housing Choice Voucher program, which pays a large portion of the rents and utilities of about 2.1 million households. The U.S. Department of Housing and Urban Development manages Section 8 programs.

The **Housing Choice Voucher Program** provides "tenant-based" rental assistance, so a tenant can move from one unit of at least minimum housing quality to another. It also allows individuals to apply their monthly voucher towards the purchase of a home, with over $17 billion going towards such purchases each year (from ncsha.org analysis – National Council of State Housing Agencies). The maximum allowed voucher amount is $2,000 a month.

The United States Department of Housing and Urban Development (HUD) and the United States Department of Veterans Affairs (VA) have created a program called Veterans Affairs Supportive Housing (VASH), or HUD-VASH, which distributes roughly 10,000 vouchers per year, at a cost of roughly $75 million per year, to eligible homeless and otherwise vulnerable U.S. armed forces veterans.–This program was created to pair HUD-funded vouchers with VA-funded services, such as health care, counseling and case management.

Under the voucher program, individuals or families with a voucher find and lease a unit (either in a specified complex or in the private sector) and pay a portion of the rent. Most households pay 30 percent of their adjusted income for Section 8 housing. Adjusted income is a household's gross (total) income minus deductions for dependents under 18 years of age, full-time students, disabled persons, or an elderly household and certain disability assistance and medical expenses.

In many localities, the Public Housing Administration (PHA) waiting lists for Section 8 vouchers may be thousands of families long.

Waits of three to six years to obtain vouchers are common and many lists are closed to new applicants. Wait lists are often briefly opened (often for just five days), which may occur as little as once every seven years. Some PHAs use a "lottery" approach, where there can be as many as 100,000 applicants for 10,000 spots on the wait list, with spots being awarded on the basis of weighted or non-weighted lotteries. Priority is sometimes given to local residents, the disabled, veterans and the elderly. There is no guarantee that anyone will ever receive a spot on the list.

HOW ABOUT GETTING THESE PEOPLE OFF THE PORCH WHO ARE DRINKING COKE AND PEPSI AND WAITING IN LONG LINES TO GET FREE PUBLIC HOUSING ASSISTANCE PROVIDED BY THE PEOPLE WHO DON'T SIT ON THE PORCH. WHEN I REFER TO THESE PEOPLE ON THE PORCH I MEAN WHITE, BLACK, HISPANIC, ARAB IMMIGRANTS OR ANY OTHER RACE. I DIDN'T WANT TO EXCLUDE ANYONE.

Congressional Funding

Not including Social Security and Medicare, Congress allocated almost $717 billion in Federal funds, plus $210 billion in State funds ($927 billion total), for means-tested welfare programs in the United States, of which half was for medical care and roughly 40 percent for cash, food and housing assistance. Some of these programs include funding for public schools, job training, SSI benefits and Medicaid.-As of 2011, the public social spending-to-GDP ratio in the United States was below the OECD (Organization for Economic Cooperation and Development) average. Roughly half of this welfare assistance, or $462 billion, went to families with children, most of which are headed by single parents. **OH BOY!**

GET HELP TODAY — You don't have to go it alone. Experts from HUD-approved housing counseling agencies work in your best interest at no cost to you. For more information about available programs and guidance on your options, call **888-995-HOPE™ (4673)**. Call 24 hours a day, 7 days a week, 365 days a year for help in more than 170 languages.

WHO'S AT FAULT

CHECK OUT THE LAST FIVE WORDS OF ABOVE SENTENCE. WHAT THE HELL? ARE WE GIVING FREE HOUSING TO EVERY TOM, DICK AND HARRY IN THE WORLD? 170 LANGUAGES. EVERY HOUR, U.S. TAXPAYERS PAID $4.87 MILLION TOWARD HOUSING ASSISTANCE IN 2016. THE 2017 FORECAST IS EVEN HIGHER. HAVE YOU HAD ENOUGH?

Federal housing subsidies are also expensive to taxpayers. In 2016, the Federal government spent $30 billion on rental subsidies for low-income households and almost $6 billion on public housing, with the majority going to single parents.

I hope you are seeing the big picture here. Until this country gets these people off the porch and working, our government will continue to go deeper in debt. It won't be long until half the people will work and the other half will sit on the damn porch and live off what you, the worker, makes.

Chapter 18

NATIONAL SCHOOL LUNCH

How Does Free Lunch Work?

Schools must serve **lunches** that meet Federal requirements and they must offer **free** or reduced-price **lunches** to eligible children. **School** food authorities can also be reimbursed for snacks served to children through age 18 in after-school educational or enrichment **programs.**

School Meal Prices

	Lunch	Breakfast
Elementary	$2.34	$1.39
Middle	$2.54	$1.47
High	$2.60	$1.51

1. What Is the National School Lunch Program?

The National School Lunch Program is a federally-assisted meal program operating in over 100,000 public and non-profit private schools and residential child care institutions. It provided nutritionally balanced, low-cost or free lunches to more than 31 million children each school day in 2012. In 1998, Congress expanded the National School Lunch Program to include reimbursement for snacks served to children in after-school educational and enrichment programs to include children through 18 years of age.

The Food and Nutrition Service administers the program at the Federal level. At the State level, the National School Lunch Program is usually administered by State education agencies, which operate the program through agreements with school food authorities.

2. How does the National School Lunch Program work?

Generally, public or nonprofit private schools of high school or under and public or nonprofit private, residential child-care institutions may participate in the school lunch program. School districts and independent schools that choose to take part in the lunch program get cash subsidies and foods from the U.S. Department of Agriculture (USDA) for each meal they serve. In return, they must serve lunches that meet Federal requirements and must offer free or reduced-price lunches to eligible children.

3. What Are the Nutritional Requirements for School Lunches?

School lunches must meet meal pattern and nutrition standards based on the latest Dietary Guidelines for Americans. The current meal pattern increases the availability of fruits, vegetables and whole grains on the school menu. The meal pattern's dietary specifications set specific calorie limits to ensure age-appropriate meals for grades K-5, 6-8, and 9-12. Other meal enhancements include gradual reductions in the sodium content of the meals (sodium targets must be reached by SY 2014-15, SY 2017-18 and SY 2022-23). While school lunches must meet Federal meal requirements, decisions about what specific foods are served and how they are prepared are made by local school food authorities.

4. How Do Children Qualify for Free and Reduced-price Meals?

Any child at a participating school may purchase a meal through the National School Lunch Program. Children from families with incomes at or below 130 percent of the poverty level are eligible for free meals. Those with incomes between 130 percent and 185 percent of the poverty level are eligible for reduced-price meals, for which students can be charged no more than 40 cents. (For the period July 1, 2013 through June 30, 2014, 130 percent of the poverty level was $30,615 for a family of four; 185 percent was $43,568.)

Children from families with incomes over 185 percent of poverty pay full price, though their meals are still subsidized to some extent. Local school food authorities set their own prices for full-price (paid) meals, but must operate their meal services as non-profit programs.

After-school snacks are provided to children on the same income eligibility basis as school meals. However, programs that operate in areas where at least 50 percent of students are eligible for free or reduced-price meals may serve all their snacks for free.

5. How Much Reimbursement Do Schools Receive?

Most of the support USDA provides to schools in the National School Lunch Program comes in the form of a cash reimbursement for each meal served. From July 1, 2014 through June 30, 2015, the basic cash reimbursement rates if school food authorities served less than 60 percent free and reduced-price lunches during the second preceding school year are:

    Free lunches: $2.93

    Reduced-price lunches: $2.53

    Paid lunches: $.28

    Free snacks: $.80

    Reduced-price snacks: $.40

    Paid snacks: $.07

School food authorities that are certified to be in compliance with the updated meal requirements will receive an additional six cents of Federal cash reimbursement for each meal served. This bonus will be adjusted for inflation in subsequent years. These above rates exclude the additional six cents. Higher reimbursement rates are also in effect for Alaska and Hawaii and for schools with high percentages of low-income students.

6. What Other Support Do Schools Get From USDA?

In addition to cash reimbursements, schools are entitled by law to receive USDA foods, called "entitlement" foods, at a value of 23.25 cents for each meal served in Fiscal Year 2012-2013. Schools can also get "bonus" USDA foods as they are available from surplus agricultural stocks.

Through Team Nutrition, USDA provides schools with technical training and assistance to help school food service staffs prepare healthful meals and with nutrition education to help children understand the link between diet and health.

7. What Types of Food Do Schools Get From USDA?

States select entitlement foods for their schools from a list of various foods purchased by USDA and offered through the school lunch program. Bonus foods are offered only as they become available through agricultural surplus. The variety of both entitlement and bonus USDA foods schools can get from USDA depends on quantities available and market prices.

A very successful project between USDA and the Department of Defense (DoD) has helped provide schools with fresh produce purchased through the DoD. USDA has also worked with schools to help promote connections with local, small farmers who may be able to provide fresh produce. Now, if you understood all the above gibberish, then you are a lot smarter than me.

8. How Many Children Have Been Served Over the Years?

In 1946, the National School Lunch Act created the modern school lunch program, though USDA had provided funds and food to schools for many years prior to 1946. About 7.1 million children were participating in the National School Lunch Program by the end of its first year,1946-47. By 1970, 22 million children were participating and by 1980, the figure was nearly 27 million. In 1990, over 24 million children ate school lunch every day. In Fiscal Year 2012, more than 31.6 million children each day got their lunch through the National School Lunch Program.

9. How Much Does the Program Cost?

The National School Lunch Program cost $11.6 billion in FY2012. By comparison, the lunch program's total cost in 1947 was $70 million; in 1950, $119.7 million; in 1960, $225.8 million; in 1970, $565.5 million; in 1980, $3.2 billion; in 1990, $3.7 billion; and in 2000, 6.1 billion.

Participation, Meals Served and Program Cost

National School Lunch Program (NSLP) Average Daily Participation

Nearly 100,000 schools/institutions serve school lunches to 30.5 million students each day, including:

19.8 million free lunches

2.2 million reduced-price lunches (student pays $.40)

8.5 million full-price lunches

5 billion lunches served annually

(Source: *USDA FY 2015 preliminary data***)**

NSLP Annual Cost

13 billion in Federal dollars, including $11.7 billion in reimbursements and $1.3 billion in commodity costs

(Source: *USDA FY 2015 preliminary data***)**

School Breakfast Program (SBP) Average Daily Participation

Over 90,000 schools/institutions serve school breakfasts to 14 million students each day, including:

11 million free breakfasts

.9 million reduced-price breakfasts (student pays $.30)

2.1 million full-price breakfasts

2.3 billion breakfasts served annually

Breakdown in Costs

The *School Lunch and Breakfast Cost Study-II* revealed the following average breakdown in costs for producing a school lunch:

Food	37%
Labor/Benefits	48%
Supplies	5%
Other, including Indirect Costs	10%
Total	**100%**

It is easy to see why school food waste goes unnoticed — America squanders just $1.2 billion via school lunch annually, a tiny slice of the estimated $218 billion in food wasted in America each year. It is estimated that about one in three American children and teenagers is overweight or obese. More disturbing is the fact that since the early 1970s, the incidence of obesity among this age group has more than tripled. **ALARMING!**

While the law forces the USDA to spend about $12 billion—or roughly double the amount allotted in 2000—on the program, kids are increasingly tossing out the fruits and vegetables now mandated to appear on cafeteria trays, regardless of their reception. A whopping 81.2 percent of schools contacted by the National School Nutrition Association reported a spike in lunches that now end up in the trash as a direct result of the nutrition regulations.

Cornell and Brigham Young Universities looked at the data and determined an astounding $4 million in food is wasted each day in lunchrooms across the nation. In one district alone, California's Los Angeles Unified School District, the program is resulting in a six-digit daily revenue loss.

Food items most frequently thrown away uneaten are salad, vegetables and fruit.

Girls throw away more food than boys.

Younger kids trash more food that older kids.

The value of wasted food is probably around $1 billion annually in the UNITED STATES.

Maybe one day we will recycle this waste and put it into a pill and that will become your next meal. With the population growth being out of control, especially in areas where the parents cannot afford children, the pill would become their lifeline. Go get-um Pharmaceutical Companies. Here come the lobbyists beating on the doors of the Senate and House members. If enough money is offered, approval could be in no time.

Chapter 19

FOOD AND DRUG ADMNISTRATION

Inspector Job Description

1. Inspects establishments where foods, drugs, cosmetics, and similar consumer items are manufactured, handled, stored, or sold to enforce legal standards of sanitation, purity and grading. Visits specified establishments to investigate sanitary conditions and health and hygiene habits of persons handling consumer products.

2. Collects samples of products for bacteriological and chemical laboratory analysis.

3. Informs individuals concerned of specific regulations affecting establishments.

4. Destroys subgrades or prohibits sale of impure, toxic, damaged or misbranded items.

5. Questions employees, vendors, consumers and other principals to obtain evidence for prosecuting violators.

6. Ascertains that required licenses and permits have been obtained and are displayed.

7. Prepares reports on each establishment visited, including findings and recommendations for action.

8. May negotiate with marketers and processors to effect changes in facilities and practices where undesirable conditions are discovered that are not specifically prohibited by law.

9. May grade products according to specified standards.

10. May test products using variety of specialized test equipment, such as ultraviolet lights and filter guns.

11. May investigate compliance with or violation of public sanitation laws and regulations and be designated Sanitary Inspector.

As of May 2011, the median annual salary for a food inspector was **$36,150 per year**, or $17.38 hourly. The median salary is a demarcation line. Half of all the food inspectors in the United States earn more than the median wage and half earn less.

Currently, the middle 50 percent of health inspectors earned annual salaries between **$33,640** and **$56,066**. The highest ten percent earned annual salaries of more than **$66,275**. A career as a health inspector is a great choice for people interested in ensuring the health and safety of work environments.

Drug Inspector Salaries

Average Base Salary is $84,181.

$40 is the Average Hourly Rate.

Average Bonus is $1818.

The FDA regulates more than $1 trillion worth of consumer goods, about 25 percent of consumer expenditures in the United States. This includes $466 billion in food sales, $275 billion in drugs, $60 billion in cosmetics and $18 billion in vitamin supplements. Much of these expenditures are for goods imported into the United States; the FDA is responsible for monitoring all imports.

These Pharma companies spend this kind of money and the FDA inspects these drugs. YET, SOME PATIENTS WHO SWALLOW THESE DAMN DRUGS ARE DYING OR, IN MANY CASES, ARE DESTROYING THEIR INTERNAL ORGANS. OKAY! I KNOW THAT many pills put out by these large Pharma companies are keeping many patients alive and helping to control the patient's everyday activities.

I, FOR ONE, TAKE TWO PHARMA DRUGS PER DAY FOR BLOOD PRESSURE. THE PILLS ARE WORKING OVERTIME AS I RESEARCH AND TYPE THIS INFORMATION FOR THIS BOOK. I JUST TOOK A DEEP BREATH.

The data shows that 14 drugs cost the Federal government and Medicare beneficiaries more than $1 billion each, accounting for nearly a quarter of Medicare prescription drug spending in 2013. Most of those drugs are used to treat chronic conditions that plague the elderly, including diabetes, depression, high cholesterol, blood pressure, dementia and asthma. Federal officials said they hoped that disseminating the data would lead to new revelations about the prescribing patterns of doctors and for particular drugs.

The brand drug Nexium, used to treat heartburn, acid reflux and related stomach ailments, cost the most: $2.5 billion for 1.5 million Medicare patients, who filled 8 million prescriptions and refills. The total cost included what was paid by Medicare, beneficiaries and third-party groups, such as supplemental health plans. The cost covered not just the drug ingredients, but also sales tax and dispensing fees. It did not, however, include sometimes substantial manufacturer rebates. The drug makers' trade group warned that that omission distorted the actual cost.

The most frequently prescribed drug was Lisinopril, a generic used to treat high blood pressure and help patients survive after heart attacks. The drug was prescribed or refilled nearly 37 million times by more than seven million Medicare beneficiaries, at a cost of $307 million.

The most expensive drug per prescription was Carbaglu, a man-made enzyme used to treat people with high ammonia levels in the blood caused by a rare disorder, according to a Kaiser Health News analysis of the data. The drug was dispensed only 24 times, but at nearly $60,000 per claim, it cost the government $1.4 million.

Total Medicaid spending for outpatient prescription drugs reflects the amount paid to pharmacies, as well as any rebates the program receives from drug manufacturers. In fiscal year 2014, Medicaid spent approximately $42 billion on prescription drugs and collected about $20 billion in rebates, for net drug spending of $22 billion. Net spending for outpatient drugs accounted for about 5 percent of total Medicaid benefit spending.

Nurse practitioners and physician assistants are writing more prescriptions, hitting a total of 576 million in 2015, more than double the number five years ago. Where is it today? I have not located the information on this topic.

Annual Causes of Death in the United States

Cause of death (Data from 2014 unless otherwise noted)	Number
All Causes	2,626,418
Major Cardiovascular Diseases [MCD]	803,227
Cerebrovascular Diseases [subset of MCD]	133,103

WHO'S AT FAULT

Essential Hypertension and Hypertensive Renal Disease [subset of MCD]	30,221
Malignant Neoplasms [Cancer]	591,699
Chronic Lower Respiratory Diseases	147,101
Accidents (Unintentional Injuries) [Total]	136,053
Motor Vehicle Accidents [subset of Total Accidents]	35,398
Alzheimer's Disease	93,541
Diabetes Mellitus	76,488
Influenza and Pneumonia	55,227
Drug-Induced Deaths	49,714
Nephritis, Nephrotic Syndrome and Nephrosis	48,146
Intentional Self-Harm (Suicide)	42,773
Septicemia	38,940
Chronic Liver Disease and Cirrhosis	38,170
Alcoholic Liver Disease [subset of Chronic Liver Disease]	19,388
Injury by Firearms	33,599
Alcohol-Induced Deaths	30,722
Parkinson's Disease	26,150
Pneumonitis Due to Solids and Liquids	18,792
Homicide	15,809
Viral Hepatitis	8,081
Human Immunodeficiency Virus (HIV) Disease	6,721
All Illicit Drugs Combined (2000)	17,000[2]
Cannabis (Marijuana)	0

2014 Data Detailing Drug-Induced Deaths, Breaking Out Specific Data for Prescription Analgesics and Heroin, as Reported by the CDC

Drug Overdose Total	47,055
Pharmaceutical Opioid Analgesics	18,893
Heroin Overdose	10,574

2010 Drug Overdose Mortality Data in Detail, Reported by Paulozzi et al.

Drug Overdose Total	38,329
Pharmaceutical Drugs	22,134
Pharmaceutical Opioid Analgesics	16,651

Adverse Drug Reactions

Adverse drug reactions are a significant public health problem in our health care system. For the 12,261,737 Medicare patients admitted to U.S. hospitals, ADRs were projected to cause the following increases: 2976 deaths, 118,200 patient-days, $516,034,829 in total charges, $37,611,868 in drug charges and $9,456,698 in laboratory charges. If all Medicare patients were considered, these figures would be three times greater.

This finding reflects about a 20 percent increase in mortality associated with an ADR in hospitalized patients. Extrapolating this finding to all patients suggests that 2976 Medicare patients a year and 8336 total patients a year die in U.S. hospitals as a direct result of ADRs; this translates to approximately 1.5 patients per hospital, per year. **Is this too high? HELL, YES!**

Big Pharma has written more than $30 billion in checks in the last ten years to resolve the government allegations, according to statistics compiled by the consumer watchdog group **Public Citizen**. Nine drug manufacturers each forked over at least $900 million from 2006 through 2015.

YES, WE, THE CONSUMER, ARE PAYING FOR THE LAWSUITS THAT HAVE HARMED OUR FELLOW AMERICANS.

In October 2015, Takeda Pharmaceuticals agreed to settle thousands of Actos bladder cancer lawsuits for **$2.4 billion**. It is one of the largest settlements in drug and device history.

Legal claims against the pharmaceutical industry have varied widely over the past two decades, including Medicare and Medicaid fraud, off-label promotion and inadequate manufacturing practices.

The pharma companies in the U.S. are being sued every day, but not one pharma company has ever lost its license to manufacture drugs that brought harm to the user.

The total number of prescriptions filled in 2016 reached 4,065,175,064.

Nearly **70** percent of Americans are on at least one prescription drug and more than half take two, according to Mayo Clinic and Olmsted Medical Center researchers. Antibiotics, antidepressants and pain-killing opioids are the most commonly prescribed.

It is fascinating that the U.S. FDA inspections found "no evidence of systemic issues," while the European inspectors were so concerned with what they found that their regulatory body banned roughly 700 generic drugs as a result of their investigations.

The banning of 700 generic drugs in Europe should serve as a wake-up call for Americans. Physicians, pharmacists and patients in the U.S. deserve the same protection that European regulators provide their citizens.

Under fire for spending so much on advertising, drug makers are doubling down. **Even as politicians and physicians press for strict limits on prescription drug ads, the pharmaceutical industry is pouring billions into new TV and print campaigns. Ad spending soared more than 60 percent in the last four years, hitting $5.2 billion last year. And there's no sign of it slowing. On the**

contrary: Nine prescription drugs are on pace to break $100 million worth of TV ad time this year.

When we're bombarded with drug ads, it can be easy to forget just how unusual the practice is. The U.S. and New Zealand are the only countries where drug makers are allowed to market prescription drugs directly to consumers.

Chapter 20

FEDERAL INCOME TAX

Flat Tax

A flat tax is exactly what it sounds like: A consistent tax rate applied to all tax brackets. A true flat tax would mean, as Dr. Ben Carson explained, that everyone would pay the same tax rate regardless of income. (He suggested ten percent, since that "works for God.") Flat taxes are usually imposed on wages only; meaning that there is no tax on capital gains or investments. Our income tax forms are about as complicated as a Chinese jig saw puzzle. Most people have to get help from an accountant or professional tax preparer just to make sure they are paying enough tax. This also ensures they are not paying too much tax.

The U.S. government collects about **$4.6 trillion** through income and payroll taxes, yearly. Income tax is where the government collects the most tax: In Federal, State, and Local income tax, they will collect about **$2.6 trillion** in 2017.

An estimated 45.3 percent of American households, or roughly 77.5 million, will pay no Federal individual income tax, according to data for the 2015 tax year from the Tax Policy Center, a nonpartisan, Washington-based research group. (Note that this does not necessarily mean they will not owe their State's income tax.) In this group, you have the retired, disabled, handicapped and people living in poverty or on public assistance (welfare). The problem is most of the welfare people could be working, but stay home on the porch as long as the rest of us pay them to do so.

The flat tax would eliminate this problem and the government would take in more money. The larger problem comes when the U.S. Government spends more than they take in.

Wealthy people pay nearly 87 percent of all Federal individual income tax in America.

Income level	Share of total Federal individual income tax paid	Average income tax bill per person
Lowest 20 percent	-2.2%	-$643
Second lowest 20%	-1.7%	-$621
Middle income	4.2%	$1,743
Second richest 20 percent	12.9%	$6,285
Richest 20 percent	86.8%	$50,176

Source: Tax Policy Center

The top one percent of Americans, who have an average income of more than $2.1 million, pay 43.6 percent of all the Federal individual income tax in the U.S.; the top 0.1 percent—just 115,000 households, whose average income is more than $9.4 million—pay more than 20 percent of it. Yet the Democrats are complaining the rich are getting richer.

What is a 'Progressive Tax'?

A progressive tax is a tax that takes a larger percentage from high-income earners than it does from low-income individuals. The U.S. income tax system is considered progressive. In 2016, individuals who had under $9,275 of taxable income paid ten percent in income tax, while taxpayers earning more than the benchmark cutoff of $415,050 fell into tax brackets with rates up to 39.6 percent.

No matter how much we, the taxpayers, pay or not pay, the Federal Government has always and, until something changes, will continue to spend much more than they take in. Now, if all individuals did the same as the government does, just think where this country would be. My generation was taught to achieve being debt free. Most of us Americans owe money, either for housing, automobile, credit card, tuition, student loans, personal loans, etc. It has become a way of life. Today, with interest rates being extremely low, borrowing is the lifeline of our country. You can buy a car, furniture, etc. at zero percent interest for several months. So, the consumer has piled on debt. This scenario continues to enhance a phony economy at the consumers' expense.

OUR GOVERNMENT, DEMOCRATS AND REPUBLICANS, ARE DECIDING THIS WEEK ON BALANCING THE BUDGET. WHAT A JOKE! MORE DEBT DUMPED ON THE TAXPAYER. THE PEOPLE ON THE PORCH DON'T CARE WHAT THE GOVERNMENT DOES, AS LONG AS THEY CONTINUE TO RECEIVE FREE FOOD, CLOTHING, HOUSING, ETC. AND LET US NOT FORGET THE PEPSI AND COKE.

Chapter 21

CONSUMER DEBT

Average Credit Card Debt in America

The mean credit card debt of U.S. households is approximately $5,700, according to the most recent data from the Survey of Consumer Finances by the U.S. Federal Reserve. This information comes from data collected through year 2013 and represents the most reliable measure of credit card indebtedness in the United States. The "mean amount of credit card debt" considers balances that Americans above the age of 18 have, on average, throughout the year.

Another method for estimating average credit card debt is to look only at indebted households, excluding those who pay their balances in full on a monthly basis. To obtain this figure, we looked at data reported by the Federal Reserve for Outstanding Revolving Debt. We then divided that number by the number of card-carrying households each year. As of March 2016, the average credit card debt for these households amounted to $16,048.

Debt is a way of life for Americans, with overall U.S. household debt increasing by 11 percent in the past decade. At the end of 2016, the average household with credit card debt had balances totaling $16,748, and the average household with any kind of debt owed $134,643, including mortgages.

While "don't spend above your means" will always be sound advice, Nerd Wallet's annual survey of household debt and its costs makes clear that increasing debt loads are not just a case of lifestyle creep. The rapid growth in medical and housing costs dwarf income growth, making it challenging for many families to make ends meet without leaning on credit cards and loans.

But, this doesn't mean Americans are doomed to be indebted for life. Careful spending and steady debt eradication can go a long way toward getting people to financial freedom.

WHO'S AT FAULT

Before we begin getting rid of our debt, it is important to know how much we are working with. Here is what the typical household is carrying, as well as total consumer debt balances in the U.S.:

	Total owed by average U.S. household carrying this type of debt	Total debt owed by U.S. consumers
Credit cards	$16,748	$779 billion
Mortgages	$176,222	$8.48 trillion
Auto loans	$28,948	$1.16 trillion
Student loans	$49,905	$1.31 trillion
Any type of debt	$134,643	$12.58 trillion

Debt balances are current as of Q4 2016; figures are updated quarterly by the Federal Reserve.

REMEMBER THE INTEREST CHARGES

The Cost of Debt

The average household with credit card debt pays a total of $1,292 in credit card interest per year. This could increase to $1,309 if the Federal Reserve votes on a rate hike of a quarter of a percentage point.

The population that is reaching retirement age should be shrinking their debt load until they become almost debt free. Retirement individuals should only have home loans and automobile loans.

A recent survey of 100 major U.S. credit cards found that consumers who fall two months behind on their credit card payments, face an average penalty interest rate of 28.45 percent. So, say you carry a $6,000 balance on your card charging 11.82 percent, the average APR. At the 28.42 percent penalty APR, you would have to pay nearly $1,000 extra in interest per year.

In 2014 alone, American Express made a net interest income of approximately $5.8 billion! This is your money folks. Only 35 percent of credit card users do not carry a balance. They pay off their bill every month, like you're supposed to.

How Many People in the U.S. Have a Credit Card?

Federal Reserve data released in 2014, for example, found 72 percent of consumers had at least one credit card. Using the Census Bureau estimate of 235 million adult consumers in the U.S., that means there are about **167 million American** adults with at least one credit card.

What Percent of People Are in Debt?

Only **20 percent** of Americans are free from any form of debt. The most common variety is mortgage debt (**44 percent**), followed by unpaid credit card balances (**39 percent**), car loans (**37 percent**) and student loans (**21 percent**).

In the year 2000, over half of the households in America had credit card debt. Since then, the average credit card debt rose from $5,048 to $7,697. This means the average American holds 52 percent more debt today than they did a decade ago.

REMEMBER, IF YOU GET IN OVER YOUR HEAD, THE DEBT PROBLEM GOES FROM BAD TO REALLY BAD IN A FEW MONTHS. ALSO, INTEREST RATES ARE LOW TODAY ONLY BECAUSE THE FEDERAL GOVERNMENT OWES TRILLIONS OF DOLLARS AND MUST PAY INTEREST ON THEIR LOANS (EQUALS OVER A TRILLION DOLLARS PER YEAR.) WHEN THE NATIONAL DEBT STARTS TO SHRINK, YOUR INTEREST RATES WILL HEAD TOWARD THE SKY. CAN YOU AFFORD IT?

Chapter 22

THE FEDERAL BUREAU OF INVESTIGATION

The Federal Bureau of Investigation is the domestic intelligence and security service of the United States, which simultaneously serves as the nation's prime federal law enforcement agency.

Founded: July 26, 1908, United States of America

Motto: Fidelity, Bravery, Integrity

First director: J. Edgar Hoover

Jurisdiction: Federal government of the United States

Founders: J. Edgar Hoover, Charles Joseph Bonaparte, Theodore Roosevelt

Operating under the jurisdiction of the U.S. Department of Justice, the FBI is concurrently a member of the U.S. Intelligence Community and reports to both the Attorney General and the Director of National Intelligence. A leading U.S. counterterrorism, counterintelligence and criminal investigative organization, the FBI has jurisdiction over violations of more than 200 categories of Federal crimes.

Although many of the FBI's functions are unique, its activities in support of national security are comparable to those of the British MI5 and the Russian FSB. Unlike the Central Intelligence Agency (CIA), which has no law enforcement authority and is focused on intelligence collection overseas, the FBI is primarily a domestic agency, maintaining 56 field offices in major cities throughout the United States and more than 400 resident agencies in lesser cities and areas across the nation. At an FBI field office, a senior-level FBI officer concurrently serves as the representative of the Director of National Intelligence.

In fiscal year 2012, the Bureau's budget totaled approximately $8.12 billion.

The FBI's main goal is to protect and defend the United States, to uphold and enforce the criminal laws of the United States and to provide leadership and criminal justice services to federal, state, municipal, and international agencies and partners.

Currently, the FBI's top priorities are:

1. Protect the United States against foreign   intelligence operations and espionage.
2. Protect the United States against cyber-based attacks and high-technology crimes.
3. Combat public corruption at all levels.
4. Protect civil rights.
5. Combat transnational/national criminal organizations and enterprises.
6. Combat major white-collar crime.
7. Combat significant violent crime.
8. Support federal, state, local and international partners.
9. Upgrade technology to enable and further the   successful performances of its missions as stated above.

Indian reservations

The Federal government has the primary responsibility for investigating and prosecuting serious crimes on Indian Reservations.

There are 565 Federally-recognized, American Indian Tribes in the United States, and the FBI has Federal law enforcement responsibility on nearly 200 Indian reservations. This Federal jurisdiction is shared concurrently with the Bureau of Indian Affairs, Office of Justice Services.

Personnel

As of December 31, 2009, the FBI had a total of 33,852 employees. That included 13,412 special agents and 20,420 support professionals, such as intelligence analysts, language specialists, scientists, information technology specialists and other professionals.

Director of the Federal Bureau of Investigation

FBI Directors are appointed by the President of the United States and must be confirmed by the United States Senate. They serve a term of office of five years, with a maximum of ten years if reappointed, unless they resign or are fired by the President. J. Edgar Hoover, appointed by Calvin Coolidge in 1924, was the longest-serving Director, holding the position until his death in 1972. In 1968, Congress passed legislation as part of the

Omnibus Crime Control and Safe Streets Act Pub.L. 90–351, June 19, 1968, 82 Stat. 197 that specified a 10-year limit, a maximum of two 5-year terms for future FBI Directors, as well as requiring Senate confirmation of appointees. As the incumbent, this legislation did not apply to Hoover, only to his successors. In 2013, Barack Obama appointed James B. Comey as FBI Director. President Trump fired Mr. Comey in May of 2017. Now, the hunt starts and the Democrats are fuming. This position should not be political.

The FBI Director is responsible for the day-to-day operations at the FBI. Along with his deputies, the Director makes sure cases and operations are handled correctly. The Director also is in charge of ensuring the leadership in any one of the FBI field offices is manned with qualified agents. Before the Intelligence Reform and Terrorism Prevention Act was passed in the wake of the September 11 attacks, the FBI Director would directly brief the President of the United States on any issues that arose from within the FBI. Since then, the Director reports to the Director of National Intelligence (DNI), who, in turn, reports to the President.

Weapons

Glock 22 pistol in .40 S&W caliber

An FBI special agent is issued a Glock Model 22 pistol or a Glock 23 in .40 S&W caliber. If they fail their first qualification, they are issued either a Glock 17 or Glock 19 to aid in their next qualification. In May 1997, the FBI officially adopted the Glock .40 S&W pistol for general agent use and first issued it to New Agent Class 98-1 in October 1997. At present, the Model 23 "FG&R" (finger groove and rail) is the issue sidearm. New agents are issued firearms on which they must qualify upon successful completion of their training at the FBI Academy. The Glock 26 in 9×19mm Parabellum, and Glock Models 23 and 27 in .40 S&W caliber are authorized as secondary weapons. Special agents are authorized to purchase and qualify with the Glock 21 in .45 ACP.

Special agents of the FBI HRT (Hostage Rescue Team), and regional SWAT teams are issued the Springfield Professional Model 1911A1 .45 ACP pistol *and* in 2016, the FBI awarded Glock a contract for new handguns. Unlike the currently issued .40 S&W chambered Glock pistols, the new Glock pistols will be chambered for 9mm. The contract is for the Glock 17M and the Glock 19M. The "M" means the Glocks were modified to meet government standards specified by a 2015 government request for proposal.

FY2016 Enacted Budget

$8,798.8 billion (35,158 positions; 3,100 intelligence analysts; 13,084 special agents)

Current Services Adjustments: -$108.0 million

Program Changes: +$811.6 million.

FY2017 Budget Request

$9,502.4 billion ((34,768 positions; 2,999 intelligence analysts; 12,894 special agents)

Change from FY2016 Enacted:

Plus $703.6 million (plus 8.0 percent; minus 390 positions; minus 101 intelligence analysts; minus 190 agents)

The FY2017 budget request proposes a total of $9.5 billion in direct budget authority to carry out the FBI's national security, criminal law enforcement and criminal justice services missions. The request includes a total of $8.7 billion for salaries and expenses, which will support 34,768 positions (12,894 special agents, 2,999 intelligence analysts, and 18,875 professional staff) and $783.5 million for construction. A few pages back FY 2012 budget stood at $8.12 billion. This is a meager $380 million more.

WHO'S AT FAULT

IT IS SIMPLY AMAZING TO ME HOW THE NUMBERS PUT OUT BY OUR GOVERNMENT ARE ALWAYS MILLIONS OR BILLIONS, WITH THE OCCASIONAL TRILLION THROWN IN THERE. THEY TREAT THESE NUMBERS LIKE MINNOWS IN A LARGE RIVER.

Nine program enhancements totaling $873.8 million are proposed to meet critical requirements and close gaps in operational capabilities, including $646 million for construction of the new FBI Headquarters building **(REALLY!)**, $85.1 million to enhance cyber investigative capabilities, $19.9 million to mitigate threats from foreign intelligence services and insider threats, $38.3 million for operational technology investments related to the Going Dark initiative, $6.8 million to add transnational organized criminals to watch lists, $27 million to leverage Intelligence Community Information Technology Enterprise components and services within the FBI, $8.2 million to enhance surveillance capabilities, $35 million to improve the timeliness and accuracy of National Instant Criminal Background Check System (NICS) services, and $7.4 million for operation and maintenance costs of the new Biometrics Technology Center.

WE SPEND BILLIONS OF DOLLARS AND, YET, WE HAVE DONE VERY LITTLE TO KEEP MR. BAD GUY OUT OF OUR COUNTRY. SANCTUARY CITIES ARE SPRINGING UP AS I WRITE THIS BOOK. DEMOCRATS RANTING AND RAVING ABOUT HELPING OUT THE REFUGEES FROM FOREIGN COUNTRIES. THE LIST GOES ON AND ON AND WE, THE VOTER, SIT BACK AND WATCH OUR ONE-TIME GREAT COUNTRY GO DOWN THE SEWER. GET OFF YOUR BUTT AND WRITE YOUR CONGRESSMAN AND SENATOR.

Overall, the FY2017 request represents an increase of $703.6 million over the FY2016 enacted levels, including an additional $229.1 million for salaries and expenses and $646 million for construction. The above is a portion of the budget request from Director James B. Comey's mouth on Feb. 25th 2016.

Chapter 23

THE CENTRAL INTELLIGENCE AGENCY

The Central Intelligence Agency was created in 1947, with the signing of the **National Security Act** by President Harry S. Truman. The Act also created a Director of Central Intelligence (DCI) to serve as head of the United States intelligence community; act as the principal adviser to the President for intelligence matters related to the national security; and serve as head of the Central Intelligence Agency. **The Intelligence Reform and Terrorism Prevention Act of 2004** amended the National Security Act to provide for a Director of National Intelligence, who would assume some of the roles formerly fulfilled by the DCI, with a separate Director of the Central Intelligence Agency.

Today's CIA

The CIA is an independent agency responsible for providing national security intelligence to senior U.S. policymakers. The Director of the Central Intelligence Agency (D/CIA) is nominated by the President, with the advice and consent of the Senate. The Director manages the operations, personnel, and budget of the Central Intelligence Agency.

The CIA is separated into five basic components: The **Directorate of Operations, the Directorate of Analysis, the Directorate of Science and Technology, the Directorate of Support and the Directorate of Digital Innovation.** They carry out "the intelligence cycle," the process of collecting, analyzing, and disseminating intelligence information to top U.S. government officials.

Additionally, the D/CIA has several staffs that deal with **public** affairs, human resources, protocol, congressional affairs, legal issues, information management and internal oversight.

CIA's Responsibilities

The CIA's primary mission is to collect, analyze, evaluate and disseminate foreign intelligence to assist the President and senior U.S. government *policymakers in making decisions relating to national* security. This is a very complex process and involves a variety of steps.

First, the CIA has to identify a problem or an issue of national security concern to the U.S. government. In some cases, the CIA is directed to study an intelligence issue—such as what activities terrorist organizations are planning, or how countries that have biological or chemical weapons plan to use these weapons—then they look for a way to collect information about the problem.

There are approximately 21,525 employees working at the CIA. This Federal department is hush- hush on what they do, their budget, how many are employed and what those employees do. I understand the reasons for keeping everyone in the dark. What I don't understand is what have they accomplished in the last twenty years. Drugs are running rampant throughout our country; terrorists are still walking on our land in almost every State and large city. Heroin is everywhere and is currently at epidemic stages. People are dying from overdoses on the streets throughout our nation. My other question: Is our nation in the path of a nuclear bomb? Even if the CIA knows what our country is up against and they inform the powers to be, what will our government leaders do about the situation after they learn of the problem? One party will want to destroy the enemy and the other party will want to wait and see.

With over 21,000 employees, it must be very difficult to keep all the information behind closed doors.

In my last fifty years of living in the U.S., I have come to the conclusion that our government reacts when the NEWS MEDIA blows the lid off a serious move by our enemy. How did the information on North Korea shooting off a ballistic missile into the Pacific Ocean hit the TV stations soon after the missile was fired? The TV even had the picture of

WHO'S AT FAULT

North Korea's launch pad. Or, is that just another picture of a missile firing at some place other than North Korea?

I remember when I was stationed with the U.S. Air Force in Germany for three years during the Berlin Crisis back in the early 1960s, Russian Migs would come across the West German border. Back then, we would scramble our F-104s from Ramstein Air Force Base and escort them back to East Germany. This was a weekly occurrence. I served as a radar operator at a secluded air base, which controlled every plane in the entire European airways.

During this period, TWA and Pam Am Airways would fly to West Berlin, Germany using the Berlin Corridor, while being escorted by four F-104s. The Russian Migs were always trailing along making sure our aircraft all stayed on course. Back in the 60s we (U.S. troops) called it a game, but the news media sold millions of copies of print newspapers informing the readers we were at stage one war with Russia.

The CIA was busy back then doing what we will never know, but I would rather have The CIA on our side than on the other side. Remember, regardless of what little we know about the CIA, they are usually in harm's way searching out our enemies. Believe me, you will sleep much better knowing the CIA is on call 24 hours a day, seven days per week, 365 days per year. You need to pray every day they all come home safely. I mentioned—**EVERY DAY YOU SHOULD PRAY FOR EVERYONE WHO RISKS THEIR LIVES TO PROTECT US.**

Chapter 24

FEDERAL AVIATION ADMINISTRATION

The **Federal Aviation Administration (FAA)** of the United States is a national authority with powers to regulate all aspects of civil aviation. These include the construction and operation of airports, the management of air traffic, the certification of personnel and aircraft and the protection of U.S. assets during the launch or reentry of commercial space vehicles.

In 1967, a new U.S. Department of Transportation (DOT) combined major Federal responsibilities for air and surface transport. The Federal Aviation Agency's name changed to the Federal Aviation Administration as it became one of several agencies (e.g., Federal Highway Administration, Federal Railroad Administration, the Coast Guard and the Saint Lawrence Seaway Commission) within the DOT (albeit the largest). The FAA administrator would no longer report directly to the President, but would instead report to the Secretary of Transportation. New programs and budget requests would have to be approved by DOT, which would then include these requests in the overall budget and submitted to the President.

Headquarters: Washington, D.C.

Formed: August 23, 1958; 59 years ago

Annual budget: $15.96 billion (Fiscal year 2017)

This multi-billion-dollar request supports their continued focus on safety-related development projects, including runway safety area improvements, runway incursion reduction, aviation safety management and improvement of infrastructure conditions. If you have flown from various airports in the U.S. recently, you will quickly realize the concrete runways are like a wash board (used to wash clothes before machines came along) as your plane roars down the runway reaching speeds between 150 and 180 MPH. Landing is no picnic either as the pilot sets the aircraft down on the corroded runway. Bumpity Bump until the plane taxis to your concourse.

For small aircraft weighing less than 200,000 pounds, a minimum runway length of **6,000 feet** at sea level is recommended. But for international aircraft that are huge, like the Airbus A310 and Boeing 777, a runway length of at least **13,000 feet** at sea level is recommended.

Needless to say, there are entire tables of data on how fast a particular 747 must be traveling before it rotates (lifts its wheels off the ground) and pilots run the math before each takeoff. These tables can be found in the Pilot's Operating Handbook. Just to pick a random scenario —let's say you are taking off from an airport at sea level, 80°F, with 10° of flaps, in a 747-400 with General Electric CF6 engines, on a calm day with no winds, on a normal, dry runway with no upslope or downslope and the airplane weighs 350,000 pounds, gross. In that case, your airplane would rotate at 164 knots (189 MPH).

Now, let's say you are taking off from an airport at 6,000 feet above sea level (say, in Colorado), on a hot, 100° day, 20° of flaps, in a 747-400 with GE CF6 engines, with a 10-knot tailwind, on a wet runway with a two percent downslope and the airplane is at max gross weight (370,000 pounds). In that case, your airplane would rotate at 182 knots (209 MPH).

FAA Scrambles to Hire Controllers

More than 35 years after President Ronald Reagan fired 11,000 air traffic controllers who had gone on strike in the midst of a bitter labor battle, the FAA still faces periodic waves of shortages. For the first time in seven years, however, the FAA is poised to catch up with recruiting efforts, at least in the near term: The agency is on track to hire 1,781 new air traffic controllers before the end of December 2017. No reports available for current year 2017.

More than 14,000 Federal air traffic controllers in airport traffic control towers, terminal radar approach control facilities and air route traffic control centers guide pilots through the system. An additional 1,292 civilian contract controllers and more than 10,000 military controllers also provide air traffic services for the NAS.

IN THE WANING DAYS OF HIS ADMINISTRATION, PRESIDENT BARACK OBAMA OFFICIALLY AUTHORIZED A

WHO'S AT FAULT

2.1 PERCENT PAY RAISE FOR FAA CIVILIAN EMPLOYEES IN 2017. SOCIAL SECURITY RECEIVED NOTHING FOR 2017.

The overall health of the U.S economy is highly dependent on the aviation industry. Civil aviation contributes roughly $1.5 trillion annually to the national economy and constitutes 5.4 percent of the gross domestic product. Aviation generates more than 11.8 million jobs, with earnings of $459 billion. The aerospace sector is a vital element in the country's balance of trade.

How Do You Become an Air Traffic Controller?
There are two ways to become an air traffic controller with the FAA. The first option is to gain military experience as an air traffic controller. The second is to complete an aviation degree at a college or university through the FAA's Air Traffic Collegiate Training Initiative program.

To say the least, it is a stressful job, especially at busy airports, such as JFK or Atlanta. As previously mentioned, I served as an Air Traffic Controller while stationed in Germany.

Chapter 25

EXECUTIVE, LEGISLATIVE AND JUDICIAL BRANCHES

The judicial branch oversees the court system of the U.S. Through court cases, the judicial branch explains the meaning of the Constitution and laws passed by Congress. The **Supreme Court** is the head of the judicial branch. The nine justices meet in the U.S. Supreme Court building in Washington, D.C.

Article III of the Constitution of the United States guarantees that every person accused of wrongdoing has the right to a fair trial before a competent judge and a jury of one's peers.

Where the Executive and Legislative branches are elected by the people, members of the Judicial Branch are appointed by the President and confirmed by the Senate. Federal judges can only be removed through impeachment by the House of Representatives and conviction in the Senate. Judges and justices serve no fixed term—they serve until their death, retirement, or conviction by the Senate. By design, this insulates them from the temporary passions of the public and allows them to apply the law with only justice in mind, and not electoral or political concerns. **YEAH, RIGHT!**

Salaries as of January, 2006

President	$400,000
Vice President	$212,100
Speaker of the House	$212,100
House Majority & Minority Leaders	$183,500
House/Senate Members & Delegates	$165,200
Chief Justice, Supreme Court	$212,100

Associate Justices, Supreme Court $203,000

Salaries as of January, 2017

President	$400,000
Vice President	$230,700
Speaker of the House	$223,500
House Majority & Minority Leaders	$193,400
House/Senate Members & Delegates	$174,000
Chief Justice, Supreme Court	$263,300
Associate Justices, Supreme Court	$251,800

Chapter 26

BUREAU OF LAND MANAGEMENT

The Bureau of Land Management (BLM) is an agency within the United States Department of the Interior that administers more than 247.3 million acres of public lands in the United States, which constitutes one-eighth of the landmass of the country.

President Harry S. Truman created the BLM in 1946 by combining two existing agencies: the General Land Office and the Grazing Service. Most BLM public lands are located in these 12 western states: Alaska, Arizona, California, Colorado, Idaho, Montana, Nevada, New Mexico, Oregon, Utah, Washington and Wyoming.

When the Wild Horse and Burro Act was passed in the 1970s, approximately 25,000 wild horses could be found nationwide. Today, the BLM is attempting to manage the 58,000 animals that are on the western rangelands—more than twice as many as is sustainable for these areas—while also seeking to find homes for the roughly 48,000 horses and burros that have already been removed from the range and are living on leased pastures or in corrals. The costs of this program are substantial and unsustainable.

DIDN'T THEY THINK HORSES AND BURROS HAVE SEX? BUT, THEN, HOW WOULD A CITY MAN KNOW ANYTHING ABOUT HORSES. I GREW UP ON A FARM.

The agency projects that the cost of caring for a horse in a corral facility is nearly $50,000 over the life of the animal. This situation has created very serious challenges to effective cost management.

HAVE YOU EVER HEARD OF SUCH HORSE MANURE IN YOUR LIFE? A HORSE LIVES TO ITS MID-TWENTIES, MAYBE. THAT FIGURES OUT TO BE OVER $2500 PER YEAR, PER HORSE. I SAY HORSE SENSE MAKES MORE SENSE. WHAT ABOUT BIRTH CONTROL PILLS?

WHO'S AT FAULT

The FY2017 budget request supports new, innovative efforts to secure safe and cost-effective placement for un-adopted animals, which will work in tandem with more proactive efforts beginning in 2016 to better manage the overpopulation problem. In addition to expanding use of contraceptives and spay and neuter treatments, the BLM is proposing legislation to better facilitate the transfer of animals to other public entities, including local, State and Federal government agencies. The BLM's proactive efforts in 2016 and 2017 are designed to begin addressing the severe overpopulation via increased adoptions and better herd management and will ultimately save money for American taxpayers by avoiding the significant costs of holding animals over the long-term.

In the 2016 Omnibus Appropriation Act, Congress supported a $45 million requested increase to allow BLM to begin implementation of the new sage grouse conservation plans and ramp up on the ground restoration and monitoring activities in support of sage-steppe habitat conservation.

The 2017 budget request includes an additional $14.2 million within Wildlife Management to expand BLM conservation efforts for sage-grouse habitat. Integral to the success of this effort is a $5 million requested increase to support implementation of the recently released National Seed Strategy. With these requests, BLM's resources dedicated to sage-grouse conservation will total $79.2 million and represent a critical investment in preserving Western values and economies.

The budget request also includes a $6.9 million increase in Resource Management Planning, Assessment and Monitoring to support implementation of the BLM's geospatial strategy. The BLM's Enterprise Geospatial Information System (EGIS) aggregates and displays data across boundaries to capture ecological conditions and trends, natural and human influences and opportunities for resource conservation, restoration, development and partnering. The BLM geospatial proposal is integrated within the Department's growing enterprise GIS capabilities and serves as a critical component of the Department's corporate geospatial strategy.

The 2017 President's budget request for the BLM includes a $13.6 million increase for National Conservation Lands, bringing program funding to an historic $50.1 million level in the year following its 15th anniversary. Resources will address high priority needs in national monuments and national conservation areas, including developing management plans for recently designated units and developing and implementing travel management plans for high use areas.

The 2017 budget also includes increases for programs funded through the Land and Water Conservation Fund, a vital component of the America's Great Outdoors initiative. The 2017 budget proposal includes a total of $88.7 million for BLM Federal land acquisition, including $44 million in requested discretionary appropriations and $44.8 million in permanent funding.

Oil and Gas Management - Oil & Gas Special Pay

The 2017 budget request includes an increase of $2.6 million to provide up to a 35 percent pay increase for employees in five critical occupational series that are funded through the Oil and Gas program.

THAT IS A NICE INCREASE! WHEN IS THE LAST TIME YOU RECEIVED A 35 PERCENT INCREASE IN YOUR SALARY?

ARTICLES WRITTEN BY SAM BLACK

WHERE HAS CUSTOMER SERVICE GONE?

Remember when customer service was your life line to rectify a problem? Now you are lucky if you reach a person. And if you do, you get someone who is either clueless as to how to resolve your problem, has the personality of a wounded groundhog, informs you the problem is yours and yours alone, has a voice that would scare a wild buffalo, smacks his or her gum while talking or has a sarcastic attitude. When you do get a friendly, cheerful, responsive, sincere, helpful person on the phone or in person, you just want to reach out and hug them. Companies today are more interested in their bottom lines than the customer's needs and wants. We recently had a new home built by what we thought was a great company. We had several problems come up and the people in charge were either unresponsive, disrespectful or blurted out "your thirty days are up." The lady who took the phone calls and tried to help was very nice, helpful, and sincere, but trapped in the greedy web of her bosses.

I want to mention a couple of companies we dealt with in order to get our new home completed. CRA, Venice, FL, did the extension of our lanai and a mistake was made. I called Larry, the sales manager, and within 48 hours the problem was rectified. He then came to our home to make sure we were satisfied. Dan's Fans, Bradenton, extremely helpful in selecting our ceiling fans. LyteWorks, Bradenton, FL, also very helpful. Vickie, South Lake Design, Sarasota, FL, went above and beyond in assisting us with the selecting, ordering and installing of our window treatments and backsplash. No, I'm not going to mention the builder. Remember—before signing any papers, you need to investigate by asking homeowners if they are satisfied.

THE TOILET BOWL

The toilet is about to be flushed. We, the hard-working taxpayers and/or seniors who have paid dearly for many years, are floating around in the bottom of the toilet. The majority of our citizens and non-citizens are swimming around above us living off of government entitlements and we are supporting them. GOT THE PICTURE? HOW DOES IT SMELL? Now, the government debt has reached over 19 trillion dollars. According to some financial wizards, our national debt will exceed 24 trillion before Washington puts the brakes on spending. Some blame the Democrats and some blame the Republicans. If you had a couple million dollars and wanted to start a business and you wanted someone to run your business, who would you hire? A. Attorney; B. Football Coach; C. Successful, Honest Businessman with Financial and Leadership Qualities; or D. Nancy Pelosi. We have been voting for lawyers for years because they are usually the only people who run for political positions in Washington. Please read "EXTORTION," by Peter SCHWEIZER, a great non-fiction book. It will open your eyes. The two-party system causes GRIDLOCK unless we use business sense. Our government is a large business, too large. Lawyers didn't obtain an education in business, so how would they know how to solve financial problems. The laws Washington change are for their own good, not yours. How do we get rid of the lawyers in Washington? Don't reelect the ones in there and let them know your vote is going elsewhere NOW. Demand changes in our political election system. Another good read is "Fatal Serum," by Sam Black, a fiction novel which can be read by any e-reader over 18. One more book to read now is "GODLESS AMERICA," by Todd Starnes. Let's end the Toilet Bowl.

THE VIRUS

This country has a virus, a virus that has affected the brains, hearts and souls of over 50 percent of our population. This virus has been around for over twenty years. Don't worry, it will not affect everyone, but some people have died from the virus. The symptoms of this virus are: HIGH BLOOD PRESSURE, IRRITABLE BOWELS, HEART BURN, NAUSEA, WORRY AND DEPRESSION. Doctors and drug companies have no cure for this virus. The only cure is for our political leaders to look in the mirror and then abide by the Constitution and the Declaration of Independence. So Help Me GOD. JUSTICE FOR ALL. STOP the CORRUPTION; STOP the DECEIVING PRACTICES; STOP BORROWING MONEY; STOP TALKING in CIRCLES; STOP PAYING PEOPLE NOT TO WORK and finally, STOP LYING to the AMERICAN PEOPLE. REMEMBER WE ARE WATCHING YOU.

TROUBLE AHEAD

Florida is in the midst of starting another boom cycle. A big problem looms ahead! Who's going to do the work? Contractors are squirming to find qualified workers. WHY? Too many people sitting on the porch in a rocking chair waiting for the next government check to arrive. No, it has nothing to do with the color of one's skin. Our government is to blame for giving away money and EBT cards to people who can still work and can find work. We have millions in our country who are collecting disability checks that can move around much better than this writer in his seventh decade.

Our education system in this country is a disgrace to our society. WHY? They expect every child coming out of high school to go to college. WRONG! These students, or 34.1 percent that are not heading for college, are swimming around wondering what to do. ANSWER! More schools teaching trades: welding, electrical, plumbing, carpentry, beauticians, truck drivers, clerical, etc. The course would be funded by the government, but has to be paid back without any exceptions, unless death or total disability. No sitting on the porch; no breathing someone else's air while others are paying him or her to do nothing. NOBODY GETS OUT OF HIGH SCHOOL WITHOUT A DIPLOMA REGARDLESS OF HOW LONG IT TAKES THEM. When our education system sends these kids out on the street without a diploma, they are going two places: jail or the porch. Either place is costing taxpayers billions. The average salary of most construction jobs is $37,000, gross, in Florida, without Labor Unions. WAKE UP AMERICA and force these political leaders to put people back to work. OVER 27 percent of our population over 18 are not working, which DOES NOT include retirees. We are talking millions of people who are living on government programs. THERE IS A BETTER WAY!

EPILOGUE

We Need to Change Our Country

I just finished one of the best eye-opening books I have ever read. **"GOD LESS AMERICA"** by Todd Starnes. This book mentions places, names and times. **Christianity and GOD** are now being withheld from public places, public buildings, public departments, public schools, and public land and, yes, even from many of our military bases.

Our own President Obama said, "We do not consider ourselves a Christian nation anymore."

Military school children are only allowed to sing Government-approved Christmas carols because they don't want to offend others.

Evangelist Billy Graham was extensively audited by the IRS using taxpayer money, yet came up with nothing. Try auditing many of our political leaders and see what they come up with.

A large percentage of our U.S. population is made up of **SHEEP** wandering around, eating, sleeping, drinking the Kool-ade and crapping wherever they please. I grew up on a farm that raised sheep and realized at a young age that a sheep was the dumbest animal on the farm. Back in biblical times, sheep wandered around, but were directed by a shepherd. They protected them and moved them to greener pastures and watering holes. Today, they wander aimlessly, but are restricted with fences.

Obama has **NEUTERED** Christmas in the White House. Crosses and nativity scenes have been banned across this nation of ours. **WHY?** They now have even taken GOD out of TGIF and replaced it with goodness.

Our wonderful, overpaid SUPREME COURT has now ruled that a human being can marry an animal.

Pro sports ridiculed TIM TEBOW for kneeling and praying on the field, but then turned around and handed out short suspensions for those who have beaten their wives or girlfriends, or use drugs. They also turn their heads when pro athletes refuse to stand for the National Anthem. What a disgrace! The NFL commissioner is a disgrace to the sport. These players not standing with their hand on their heart while our National Anthem is being played should be put on a plane and sent to Iran.

WHO'S AT FAULT

REMEMBER: WITHOUT FAITH, YOU ARE LOST AND OUR COUNTRY WILL BE LOST UNLESS THINGS CHANGE SOON.

TERM LIMITS ARE A MUST IN WASHINGTON. GET THOSE RASCALS OUT OF WASHINGTON BEFORE THEY FIGURE OUT HOW TO REAP MORE OF OUR TAX DOLLARS.

Sources Include (but not limited to)

Aircraft Owners and Pilots Association
American Society of Civil Engineers
Center for Immigration Studies
Center for Responsive Politics
Congressional Research Service
Credit Cards.com
Drugwatch
Federal Aviation Administration
FBI Special Weapons
Federal Reserve for Outstanding Revolving Debt
Harvard University Kennedy School
Huffington Post
Investopedia
Mayo Clinic
NCAA
National Council of State Housing Agencies
National Research Council
Olmstead Medical Researchers
Organization for Economic Cooperation and Development
Pew Research Center
Stockholm International Peace Research Institute
Tax Policy Center
24/7 Wall St.
U.S. Census Bureau
U.S. Department of Agriculture
U.S. Federal Reserve
Washington Post
Wikipedia

MORE BOOKS BY SAM BLACK

Avengement

Fatal Serum

Humor to Remember

Until

www.samblackbooks.com